THE NEW

WEATHER

BOOK

MICHAEL OARD

First printing: March 1997
Revised and Updated
Ninth printing: February 2018

Master Books®
P.O. Box 726,
Green Forest, AR 72638

Master Books® is a division of the
New Leaf Publishing Group, Inc.

ISBN: 978-0-89051-861-8
ISBN: 978-1-61458-433-98 (digital)
Library of Congress Number: 2014958656

Cover and interior design: Diana Bogardus

Unless otherwise noted, Scripture quotations are from the English Standard Version of the Bible.

Please consider requesting that a copy of this volume be purchased by your local library system.

Printed in China

Please visit our website for other great titles:
www.masterbooks.com

For information regarding author interviews, please contact the publicity department at (870) 438-5288.

Photo & Illustration Credits:

Photo Credits: t-top, b-bottom, l-left, r-right, c-center

Shutterstock: Cover, pg 1, pg 2, pg 3, pg 4, pg 5, pg 6, pg 7 (2), pg 8, pg 9, pg 11, pg 12t, pg 13 (3), pg 14, pg 18-19 (9), pg 20, pg 22, pg 23 (4), pg 24 (3), pg 26 (3), pg 27 (4), pg 29t, pg 30t (2), pg 31 (2), pg 32, pg 33 (2), pg 34, pg 36, pg 37, pg 39 (2), pg 40, pg 41b, pg 44tr, pg 45t (3), pg 46t, pg 47c, pg 48, pg 52, pg 55, pg 57, pg 59c (2), pg 60, pg 61, pg 62 (2), pg 63, pg 64 t, pg 65b (2), pg 66, pg 67, pg 68, pg 69 (2), pg 73b (2), pg 76, pg 77, pg 78, pg 79b, pg 81, pg 82, pg 83, pg 84, pg 87, pg 89 (3), pg 91, pg 92, pg 93, pg 94 (4)

iStock: pg 42t

Wikimedia Commons: Images from Wikimedia Commons are used under the CC-BY-SA-3.0 license (or previous creative commons licenses) or the GNU Free Documentation License, Version 1.3. U.S.
pg 10 (NASA's Aqua/MODIS satellite), pg 42b (NWS Aberdeen, SD), pg 44tl, pg 49 (1-Ks0stm) (2-Maj. Geoff Legler) (3-TSgt Bradley C. Church) (4-Sgt. 1st Class Kendall James, Oklahoma National Guard), pg 50 , pg 58 (1-United States Marine Corps.) (2-B.L. Singley) (3-FEMA News Photo), pg 59t (Bob Epstein, FEMA News Photo), pg 71 (Frank Vincentz), pg 72 (Joe Thomissen), pg 75 (Bily slon), pg 80 (Magnus Manske)

Dreamstime: pg 12b,

Thinkstock: pg 45b, pg 85,

National Geographic Creative: pg 51b (Carsten, Peter)

NOAA: pg 15t (3), pg 41t, pg 44b, pg 47t, pg 51t, pg 54, pg 88,

NASA: pg 56, pg 64, pg 74 (Jeff Schmaltz, MODIS Rapid Response Team, NASA/GSFC)

Flickr Commons: pg 15b,

Flickr: pg 28t (dianabog), pg 73t (2) (quintanomedia)

Lloyd R. Hight: pg 16, pg 21 (2), pg 25, pg 28b, pg 29b, pg 30b, pg 35, pg 38 (3), pg 43, pg 46b, pg 53b, pg 65t, pg 79t, pg 86, pg 90

sciencesource.com: pg 53t (Paolo Koch), pg 70 (Gary Hincks)

WONDERS OF CREATION SERIES

The Geology Book	978-0-89051-281-4
The NEW Ocean Book	978-0-89051-905-9
The NEW Weather Book	978-0-89051-861-8
The Fossil Book	978-0-89051-438-2
The Cave Book	978-0-89051-496-2

The Archaeology Book	978-0-89051-573-0
The Ecology Book	978-0-89051-701-7
The NEW Astronomy Book	978-0-89051-834-2
The Mineral Book	978-0-89051-802-1

WONDERS of CREATION

multi-age format

Our best-selling Wonders of Creation Series is getting even better!

The series is being developed with an enhanced educational format and integrated with a unique color-coded, multi-skill level design to allow ease of teaching the content to three distinct levels.

How to use this book: *The New Weather Book* has been updated and developed with three skill levels in mind. These can be utilized for the classroom, independent study, or homeschool setting and also be customized per the abilities of the student.

It is recommended that every reader examine the text on the white background, as this is the basic skill level information related to the material. More proficient students and those with increased interest in the subject matter can then proceed to the more advanced concept levels. Additionally, the most advanced readers, after having read through all levels of the material, can use the upper-level material as a springboard for independent research and other educational assignments (research papers, oral reports, presentations, imaginative projects, etc.).

Level 1

The basic level is presented for younger readers and includes the various Safety Tips segments indicated by this icon:

SAFETY TIPS

Level 2

This middle level delves deeper into issues related to the weather and climate, utilizing the Words to Know in each chapter to assist with vocabulary development and comprehension.

Level 3

This upper level incorporates more advanced concepts and theories related to all subject matter included in the text, as well as unique information that will inspire additional research or learning about advancements in meteorology or specific weather-related activities.

Whether using the material as a unit study, part of a curriculum, simply a book of interest, or even a reference book for other materials, *The New Weather Book* will engage students with amazing visuals and facilitate learning through helpful charts and diagrams where needed. As always, whether discussing weather facts, history, or its many interesting features, God's place as Creator is honored within this informative study.

01 | God Created

There are days when the sun shines from a cloudless sky and warm breezes cause the leaves to flutter. Other days are gray, cloudy, and rainy. What we decide to do for the day often depends upon the weather. If it is cold and dreary on Saturday, we play inside. A heavy snow inspires us to build a snow fort. The weather also determines how we dress for the day.

Weather affects your moods. A gentle breeze and sunny skies make you cheerful. Have you noticed the bright smiles a sunny day brings, especially after bad weather? But when the wind whistles around the corners of your home or howls down your chimney, you feel anxious.

Weather affects our decisions. It determines what we wear to school. Businessmen listen to the weather report so they can plan work more effectively. If your father is a cement contractor, he needs to know if it is too cold, or too wet, to pour his cement. Airports need to know weather conditions so they can advise pilots.

Words to Know

atmosphere	latitudes
axis	nitrogen
carbon dioxide	oxygen
climate	tide

Level 1 | Level 2 | Level 3

Jesus the Creator

The Bible tells us in John 1:10 that Jesus created everything: *"He was in the world, and the world was made through him, yet the world did not know him."* The Apostle Paul says in the first chapter of the Book of Colossians that He created the atmosphere and the weather: *"For by him all things were created, in heaven and on earth, visible and invisible, whether thrones or dominions or rulers or authorities—all things were created through him and for him."* (Colossians 1:16).

God used His infinite wisdom to create this earth. From the smallest to the largest features of creation, He displays His intelligence, love, and careful attention to detail. Our world was specially created with design and purpose. In many other ways, Jesus made sure that this world would be a good home for us. For those who choose to listen, all creation shouts of His wondrous works and His love: *"For his invisible attributes, namely, his eternal power and divine nature, have been clearly perceived, ever since the creation of the world,[a] in the things that have been made. So they are without excuse."* (Romans 1:20).

When we know more about God's order in creation, we can predict the number of hours of daylight, the seasons, and the weather. His order is seen as the sun rises and sets, marking each day. Seasons have come and gone since creation. Life-sustaining rain and snow regularly water the world around us. Weather is part of the system God uses to preserve and nourish His plants and animals. In this way He makes the planet liveable for humans. It is only because God gave us an ordered planet that we can predict the weather.

Why Dangerous Weather?

Sometimes the harmony we have come to expect in nature appears out of whack. A terrible storm destroys homes and crops. Hail pelts a field of grain and destroys a farmer's crops and income within minutes. A sudden tornado crushes a mobile home. A winter blizzard ties up traffic and breaks electrical lines, causing power outages.

Have you ever wondered why God, who is so good, allows His creation to be briefly interrupted by short periods of dangerous weather? We find the answer in the Old Testament Book of Genesis. There is another principle at work in our world. It is called the sin principle. God, in the beginning declared His creation "very good." It was perfect. There was no death or sickness. The lion and the lamb were friends. Instead of the lion eating the lamb, he ate plants. Best of all, the weather was lovely everywhere. There was perfect order and harmony.

Chapter 3 of the Book of Genesis then tells how this all changed. Adam and Even were given a choice. With a little help from Satan, they disobeyed God's only command — to not eat the fruit from "the tree of the knowledge of good and evil" (Genesis 2:17). You may wonder why God gave them any command at all. For them to be best friends with God, Adam and Even needed to be free. You would not want a best friend who was forced to love you. It's difficult to have a loving relationship with someone who has no choice. God gave Adam and Eve the freedom to choose, but they wanted it all. They thought they would be like God. They chose to know both good and evil. They couldn't have it both ways because God is all good. They had to leave paradise.

The world they entered as a result of their choices was very different. They came to know evil. Animals ate each other, people died, and sometimes the weather went crazy. As the Bible says, death entered the world. Now we have good and evil living side by side. We cannot judge Adam and Eve too harshly. We very likely would have done the same thing.

God's laws are all good. If we choose to love and obey His commands, we will experience the harmony, love, and joy a good relationship with Him brings. We will also enjoy good relationships with other people. That is what God desires for us.

So we see that the world changed because of Adam and Eve's choices. As a result, we sometimes experience dangerous storms and other difficulties. But God showed us His mercy by offering us forgiveness through a Savior, Jesus. He also gave us minds so we can learn about the laws governing the weather and to predict storms.

The Anthropic Principle

God's created the universe and world just right to sustain life on earth. This is called the anthropic principle and is powerful evidence for God's existence and love for us.

God placed the moon 240,000 miles (384,000 km) away from the earth — exactly the right distance to cause small tides in the ocean. If the moon were a little closer, it would cause severe tides and flooding. If the moon were only 50,000 miles (80,000 km) away instead of 240,000 miles, the tides would cover most of the continents — twice a day! If the moon were farther away, much of the ocean would become heavily polluted. Tides mix the ocean water. The mixing helps to keep the oceans fresh by exposing more of the water to sunlight and by dispersing pollution. The amount of water in the ocean is important as well, because the oceans are large enough to dilute the pollution.

Did you know that the sun is 400 times the size of the moon, and its distance is 400 times the distance of the moon from the earth? That is why the sun and moon, the greater and lesser lights of Genesis 1:16, look the same size in the sky. This amazing fact also accounts for solar and lunar eclipses.

The earth spins on its axis at just the right speed — once around every day. If it spun slower, the light side would be too hot for life, and the dark side would be too cold. If the earth spun any faster, it would cause fierce winds to blow.

If the tilt of the earth's axis (23.5°) were smaller, the higher latitudes would be too cold, and an ice age would develop. If the tilt were greater, surface temperatures would fluctuate wildly, more so than today, making the climate more unstable. The tilt gives us our seasons. Summers are long enough for us to grow food. Winter provides a period of dormancy needed for many plants.

Ocean Tides and Currents

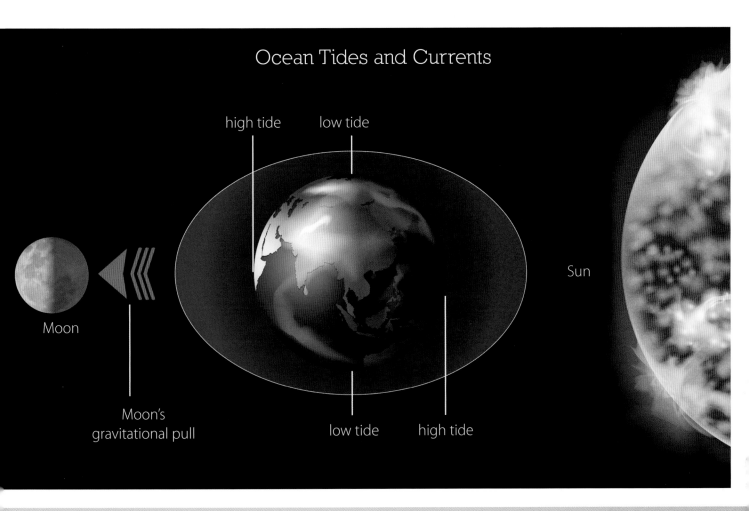

high tide   low tide

Moon

Moon's
gravitational pull

low tide   high tide

Sun

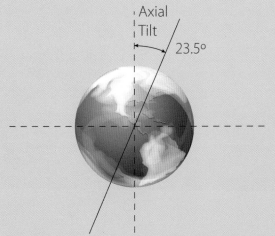

Axial
Tilt
23.5°

God placed just the right amount of water vapor and carbon dioxide in the atmosphere. Our ocean is the right size to maintain the proper balance of water vapor in the atmosphere. These gases cause the earth to act like a giant greenhouse. If there were much less of these gasses, the earth would be too cold. Although these invisible gases make up about 0.1 percent of the atmosphere, they cause the earth to be about 60°F (33°C) warmer. If there were much more of these gases, the earth would be too hot.

God put exactly the right amount of oxygen in the atmosphere. The atmosphere is composed of about 21 percent oxygen, 78 percent nitrogen, 0.9 percent argon, and about 0.1 percent water vapor and carbon dioxide. If there were more oxygen, the processes in our bodies would react too fast. More oxygen would cause fires to burn too quickly. Forest fires would rage completely out of control. If there were less oxygen in our atmosphere, processes in our bodies would operate too slowly.

The atmosphere's thickness protects us from the 20 million meteors that hit the earth each day at speeds averaging 10 miles/sec (16 km/sec). The vast majority burn up before they reach the ground. The atmosphere also absorbs practically all the harmful cosmic rays that bombard the top of the atmosphere.

God even made the earth just the right size for gravity to hold earth's water and the atmosphere in place.

02 | What Causes Earth's Weather

Weather is the momentary condition of the air. Besides temperature and precipitation, it includes wind direction and wind speed, visibility, the amount of water vapor, air pressure, cloud conditions, and air quality. Precipitation is moisture that falls from the sky in the form of rain, freezing rain, snow, hail, or drizzle. Air quality is determined by how much dust, haze, or pollution is in the air.

The weather also depends on the latitude and how close to the ocean you are. Summer temperatures are cooler in northern Europe than in southern Europe. During winter in the Northern Hemisphere, it is usually very cold in Saskatchewan, Canada, while in Texas the weather is mild. It makes a difference whether you live in Seattle, Washington, close to the ocean, or in Bismarck, North Dakota, far from the ocean at the same latitude. Seattle is kept mild by a flow of air from off the Pacific Ocean.

Words to Know

arid	low-pressure system
barometer	ice cap
condensation	meteorologist
dew point	precipitation
Doppler radar	weather balloon
equator	

Level 1	Level 2	Level 3

The Weather "Engine"

The sun is the ultimate cause of weather because of the differences in heating on the earth. This is why the sun with its differences in heating is called the weather engine. As sunlight enters the atmosphere, its rays are either absorbed by the air or reflected back to space from the white clouds. Sunlight that makes it to the ground is both absorbed and reflected. Most of the reflected light goes back into space. The sunlight absorbed at the earth's surface heats the ground. As the surface warms, it heats the atmosphere above it.

The ground and atmosphere continually lose heat by infrared radiation (invisible rays that cool the land at night). Many of these infrared rays are absorbed by the atmosphere, but those that escape into space cause the cooling. Clouds act like a blanket to keep the earth warmer at night. They absorb most of the infrared radiation and redirect some of it back to the ground. As a result, the ground and air below the clouds do not cool off much at night.

The infrared radiation cools the earth at night. When the sun comes up, the sunshine warms the ground and air. This is why the air cools at night and warms during the day. If the days are long and the nights short during summer, more heat is gained by sunshine than is lost by infrared radiation in a 24-hour period. So temperatures warm as summer approaches. It works the opposite in winter. The shorter days and longer nights result in more loss of heat in a 24-hour period. As winter comes, temperatures become colder.

The difference between daytime sunshine and nighttime infrared cooling also causes temperature differences between the tropics and polar latitudes. These temperature differences cause air pressure changes, which push the earth's winds. Air blows from high pressure to low pressure. For example, the air inside a tire is at a higher pressure than the atmosphere. There are more air molecules per cubic inch or cubic centimeter in the tire than in the atmosphere. So when you loosen the valve, the air flows out of the tire. It works the same way in the atmosphere.

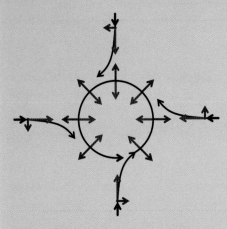

The Coriolis Force

Because of the earth spinning on its axis, air flow in the atmosphere is more complicated. The spin causes air to move to the right in the Northern Hemisphere and to the left in the Southern Hemisphere. This deflecting force on the air is called the Coriolis force. As air blows from high to low pressure, the Coriolis force causes air to circulate in a spiral around a low-pressure center. The air spirals counterclockwise around a low center in the Northern Hemisphere and clockwise in the Southern Hemisphere. Because the air is spiraling toward the center of the low, it is forced upward, forming clouds and precipitation. Practically all precipitation is formed from upward-moving air.

The Coriolis force in the Northern Hemisphere is like a disk rotating counterclockwise. Pretend you are at the center of the disk. If you throw a ball toward a target on the edge of the disk, the ball will miss to the right. It will appear that the ball was deflected to the right. What really happened was that as the ball reached the edge, the disk rotated to the left underneath the ball. It works the same in the atmosphere as the earth rotates.

A low-pressure system over Iceland spins counterclockwise due to balance between the Coriolis force and the pressure gradient force.

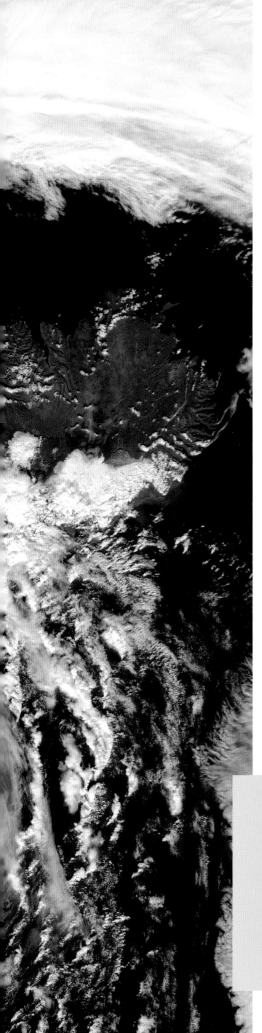

What İs the Jet Stream?

The differences in heating over the earth cause the jet stream, a ribbon of high-speed wind in the upper atmosphere. It generally moves from a westerly direction at speeds that can exceed 250 mph (400 kph) at altitudes of 6 to 12 miles (10 to 20 km).

The weather engine causes the jet stream in the middle latitudes. The jet stream meanders around the globe like a snake. The Northern and Southern Hemispheres each have a jet stream. Many important weather features are connected to the jet stream.

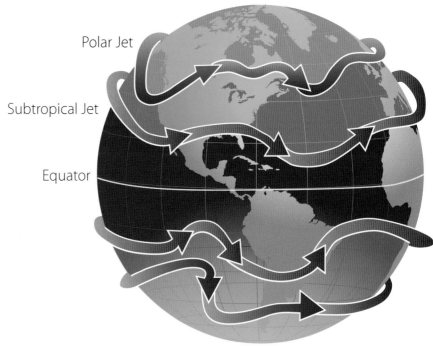

Polar Jet

Subtropical Jet

Equator

The Cause of the Jet Stream

The jet stream is caused by the difference in temperature between the tropical and polar latitudes. This north-south temperature difference causes the west wind to increase upward. The wind reaches a maximum just below the stratosphere (an upper level of the atmosphere). The stronger the temperature difference between equator and pole, the stronger the wind. Temperature differences are more during the winter and less during the summer. That is why the average speed of the jet stream is 90 mph (144 kph) during the winter and only 35 mph (56 kph) during the summer.

11

The Jet Stream Zigzags

The jet stream is constantly changing. The three globes above show the jet stream of the Northern Hemisphere at different times. The jet stream zigzags around the earth as waves. When the wind is strong, it often forms three waves. When the wind is weak, five waves are often observed. Sometimes the jet stream will split in two and reform downstream. To further complicate matters, the waves can remain stationary or they can move east or west. All these changes in the jet stream make forecasting the weather a challenge!

In the three globes above, you will notice that the jet stream is made up of waves. Within one wave, the southwest wind transports warmer air north. The northwest wind transports colder air southward. This interaction causes a storm or a low-pressure center. The storm is usually found below the southwest wind of the jet stream. A high-pressure area is generally located below the northwest wind. Associated with the storm are cold and warm fronts. The storm is guided by the jet stream's wind direction. This is why storms generally move from west to east.

Wind speed within the jet stream also varies. It may blow 75 mph (120 kph) in one area, but farther along it may blow 200 mph (320 kph). Meteorologists often think of the jet stream as a thick ribbon or a tube of air. They will draw wind speeds on a map of the world. The more lines in the tube, the faster the air.

Jet stream charts are important to weatherpersons because stormy weather can usually be found associated with certain portions of the maximum wind. If you placed a balloon in the jet stream, it would zigzag north and south, slow down and speed up. During all this commotion, the balloon would still make it around the world in about 14 days.

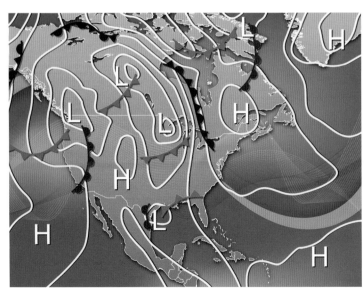

Weather Maps

If you watch on TV, or use a weather app, you will usually see a weather map displayed. This map will have low and high-pressure centers with lines drawn around them. Before the map can be drawn, however, weather observations at the same time must be taken from all over the earth.

Memory Tip: A science teacher in southern California taught his students how to remember the difference between a cold and warm front. Think of the triangles as icicles and the semicircles as blisters.

There are two types of weather observations. One type is the surface observation. Each weather station takes measurements of temperature, dew point, clouds, precipitation, pressure, and wind speed and direction. These are sent out by computer to other stations at least once an hour. If significant weather occurs, surface observations are sent out between hours.

The second type of observation is the upper air observation. This is done by weather balloons and taken twice a day, at noon and midnight Greenwich time in England. The instrument on the balloon measures the temperature, dew point, and pressure in the atmosphere up to 100,000 feet (30,500 m). A special radar tracks the balloon and provides wind direction and speed. All these observations are then plotted on maps. Weather maps used to be drawn by hand but now computers draw them.

On a surface map, lines connecting stations with equal pressure are drawn, called isobars. From these lines we find where the low pressure and high-pressure centers are. On the map you will see the location of low-pressure centers labeled with "L." Low-pressure areas are generally areas of stormy weather. High-pressure areas, labeled with an "H," are generally good weather areas. However the skies may be clear in high pressure, but temperatures may be cold in winter at mid and high latitude, like in an Arctic high that moves southward from Canada or Alaska.

You will also see weather fronts on the map. A front is a boundary between air of different temperature and moisture content. If the front is not moving, it is called a stationary front and is shown by a line with alternating triangles and semicircles. If the cold air, which is usually to the north or west, is displacing the warm air, it is a cold front and is labeled by a line with triangles. The triangles are drawn pointing in the direction the cold air is moving. If warm air is pushing out cold air, it is a warm front. A warm front is shown by a line with semicircles, the rounded part pointing in the direction of movement, which is usually northward.

weather balloon

meteorological station

Television weather forecasters often use graphic symbols.

Sunny Partly Cloudy Cloudy Rain Thunderstorms Snow Freezing Rain

L – Center of a low pressure area

H – Center of a high pressure area

⇨ – Jet Stream

Cold Front: a front in which cold air is displacing warm air.

Warm Front: a front in which warm air is displacing cold air.

Stationary Front: a front that is not moving.

Occluded Front: a front in which the cold front has caught up with the warm front, usually near a low-pressure center. The weather is similar to a cold front.

How to Make a Weather Forecast

Using weather observations, the locations of all the fronts on a weather map, and the jet stream, the weatherperson can now make a forecast. From studying the atmosphere and the many scientific processes that occur, meteorologists have developed equations. These equations are fed into one of the world's fastest computers and projected into the future. After millions of computer operations, the positions of the jet stream, the fronts, and the pressure centers are estimated in the future. This information is plotted on forecast maps at big weather centers and sent all over the world to smaller weather stations.

The weatherperson at each weather station receives lines on a map that represent the future weather pattern. He or she must then interpret these lines for his or her area. Over the years weather maps have improved. They are not perfect, however. Meteorologists do not know enough about the atmosphere, nor do they have enough observations. They need bigger and faster computers. So the weather maps still have to be interpreted. Even if the weather maps were perfect, it would be difficult to forecast the exact weather for their specific area. Weatherpeople work from lines on the map, satellite pictures, Doppler radar, lightning detection charts, and other tools to predict temperature, precipitation, wind, and cloud conditions. They also issue advisories, watches, and warnings for bad weather. Many times forecasting is easy; sometimes it is difficult. That explains why weather forecasts are sometimes incorrect.

A ground weather radar station in Italy; the radar dish sees through the surrounding dome that protects it.

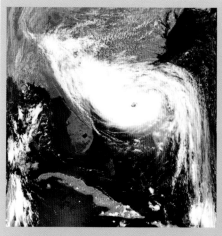

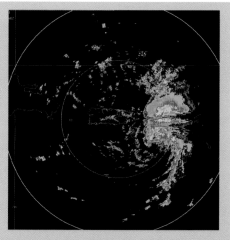

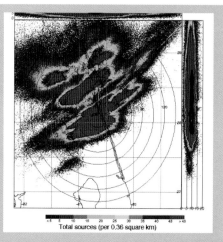

Total sources (per 0.36 square km)

Satellite Pictures

Satellite pictures have greatly aided weather forecasting. They provide locations of low-pressure systems, clouds, fronts, and other features of the atmosphere. Whereas there were no pictures over the oceans, now there are. These satellite pictures help weather forecasting models in providing exact locations.

Doppler Radar

Another tool commonly used in weather forecast is Doppler radar. Doppler radar measures by the reflection of radio waves. It not only measures the reflection off cloud drops and precipitation, it also shows the speed of the clouds and the progress of a storm. Doppler radar works on the principle that an object moving away from the radar will reflect sound waves back at a decreased frequency. Objects moving toward the radar will show an increase in frequency. Christian Doppler discovered the effect in 1842, which is why the principle is named after him.

Lightning Detection Chart

The lightning detection chart is another tool routinely used by weather forecasters. Using instruments to pick up loud sounds and trigonometry from several detectors, cloud-to-ground lightning strikes can be plotted in real time on a map. In this way, forecasters can keep track of thunderstorms and note a change in intensity.

Since the 1870s, the U.S. federal government has been involved in the collection of meteorological data. Though the name of the various agencies have changed in the last century, their mission remains. The National Oceanic and Atmospheric Administration (NOAA) is overseen by the United States Department of Commerce and is focused on scientific areas like weather, climate, conservation, marine commerce, and the oceans. The National Weather service is one component of NOAA and is responsible for collecting and distributing data, forecasts, and weather-related warnings. The Storm Prediction Center, which is tasked with assessing and issuing advance warnings for severe weather, is also part of the National Weather Service. The National Hurricane Center is a unit of the National Centers for Environmental Prediction.

The General Circulation

The differences in heating across the earth and the weather cause an average flow of air called the general circulation. Air generally rises at the equator. From there it spreads north and south. Air sinks at about 30° latitude. At that latitude it hits the ground and is forced both north and south, forming the trade winds. The air spreading back toward the equator at high altitude forms a closed circulation. Two other closed circulations are found in the middle and high latitudes of each hemisphere. The middle latitude circulation causes westerly winds at the surface, while the high latitude circulation causes easterly winds at the surface. The earth has a total of six average circulations.

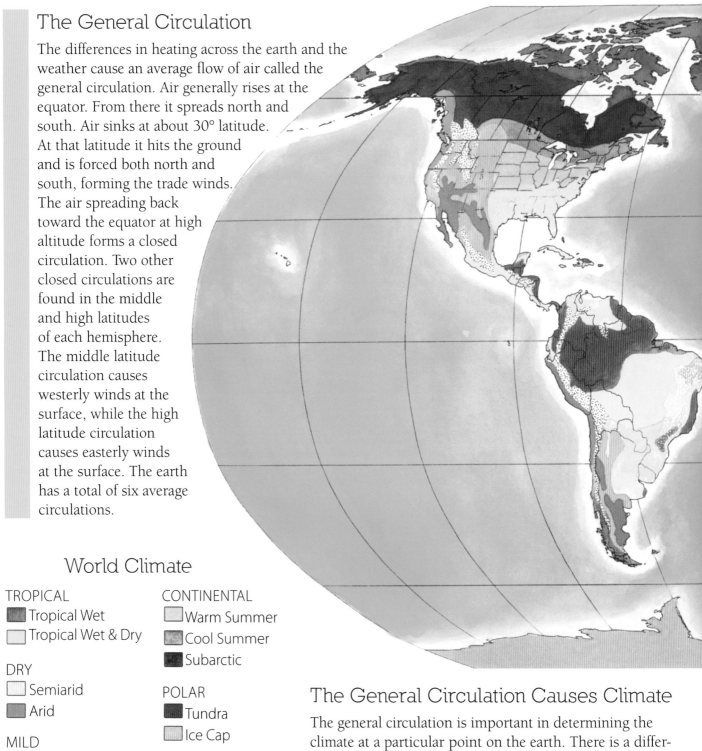

World Climate

TROPICAL
- ▨ Tropical Wet
- ☐ Tropical Wet & Dry

DRY
- ☐ Semiarid
- ▨ Arid

MILD
- ▨ Marine West Coast
- ▨ Mediterranean
- ☐ Humid Subtropical

CONTINENTAL
- ☐ Warm Summer
- ▨ Cool Summer
- ▨ Subarctic

POLAR
- ▨ Tundra
- ☐ Ice Cap

HIGH ELEVATIONS
- ▨ Highlands
- ▨ Uplands

The General Circulation Causes Climate

The general circulation is important in determining the climate at a particular point on the earth. There is a difference between climate and weather. Climate is the weather we would normally expect at any location. It is the average weather condition for a particular place at a particular time. In Death Valley, California, for example, the climate is very hot and dry during the summer. In Fairbanks, Alaska, the winters are very cold and the summers pleasantly warm. By knowing the climate, we can plan our lives better. If we know what to expect, we can be safe and comfortable even in a harsh climate.

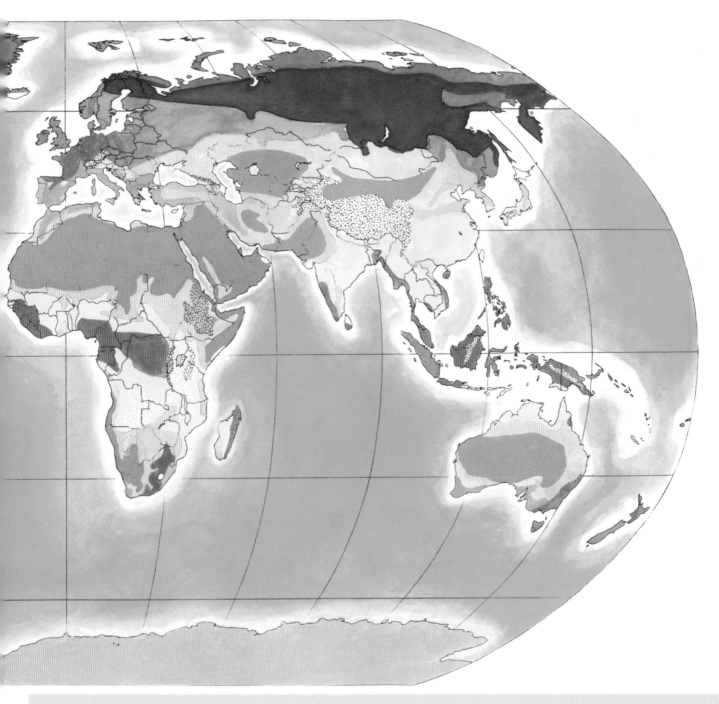

The Differences in Climate

Because of the general circulation, each place on earth experiences a different climate. Where the air generally rises, lots of precipitation is present. Sinking air, on the other hand, brings dry air downward from high in the atmosphere. As a result, it is very wet near the equator where the air rises. These are our tropical rain forests. Many of the earth's deserts are at 30° latitude where air sinks. This is why the great Sahara Desert is almost rainless. The mid-latitudes are much wetter than at 30° latitude, and the poles are cold and mostly dry.

Other variables, in addition to the general circulation, help to determine climate. A main variable is the distance from the ocean. The closer to the ocean, especially in the mid-latitudes, the wetter the climate. The farther from the ocean, the drier. The presence of mountains is also another variable. Mountains are cooler and wetter, while downwind it is drier. The general circulation, land-ocean distribution, and mountains all cause a complicated climate pattern.

Coldest

The coldest temperature ever recorded in the world was -129°F(-89°C). It was measured on July 21, 1983, at Vostok on the Antarctic Ice Sheet at 11,200 feet (3,400m) above sea level. At that temperature carbon dioxide can freeze to dry ice.

Siberia has the second-coldest record. Their record low is only -90°F (-68°C). The coldest temperature ever recorded in North America was -81°F (-63°C) at Snag, Yukon Territory, Canada.

Did you know that fresh snow reflects about 90 percent of the solar radiation (heat and light energy) back into the atmosphere? The snow surface receives so little heat that the air above it stays cold.

Hottest

The hottest temperature ever recorded was 134° F (56.7° C) on July 10, 1913 in Death Valley, California. The record had previously thought to be from El 'Azizia, Libya, on September 13, 1922 at 136.4° F (58° C). However, upon review by the World Meteorological Organization, this temperature is now considered invalid.

In January 1960, Oodnadatta, South Australia, soared to 123.3°F (50.7°C).

The place with the hottest average in the world is Dallol in Ethiopia. It is on the edge of the Sahara Desert and has an average annual temperature of 94°F (34.4°C).

Windiest

The highest recorded surface wind speed was in the May 3, 1999, Oklahoma tornado. It was measured by a portable Doppler radar at 302 mph (486 kph).

The fastest wind gust ever recorded with a wind instrument is 253 mph (407 kph) in 1996 at Barrow Island, Australia, during Typhoon Olivia. A typhoon is another name for a hurricane.

In 1934 on Mount Washington, in New Hampshire, a gust of wind was recorded at 231 mph (371 kph).

Snowiest

The most snow to fall in a one-year period is 102 feet (3,150 cm) at Mount Rainier, Washington, from February 19, 1971, to February 18, 1972.

The most snow in one season was 95 feet (2,900 cm) at Mount Baker, Washington, from July 1, 1998, to June 30, 1999.

The world record for snow depth is 39 feet (1,182 cm) measured on the slope of Mt. Ibuki in Shiga Prefecture, Japan on February 14, 1927.

Mount Rainier

Driest

Two of the driest areas of the world are the Atacama Desert in northern Chile, and the eastern Sahara Desert in Africa. Most years they do not receive any rainfall. In fact, Calama, Chile, didn't have a drop of rain from 1570 to 1971. That's 400 years without rain!

Did you know that the top of the Antarctic ice sheet normally receives only an inch (2.5 cm) of water in the form of snow each year? In fact, it is called a polar desert. Remember that Antarctica is a continent of land layered with ice. Where do you think its 10,000 feet (3,050 m) of ice could have come from, if the precipitation is this low? (See page 79.)

Lowest

The lowest air pressures on earth probably occur at the center of a tornado. It is doubtful if it could ever be measured. It would be very difficult to place a barometer at the center, and if it could be done the winds would no doubt destroy it.

Typhoon Tip had the lowest sea level air pressure ever recorded on earth; it was 25.69 inches (65.3 cm) on October 12, 1979.

Fastest

What was probably one of the fastest temperature changes happened in Spearfish, South Dakota, on January 22, 1943. At 7:30 in the morning, the temperature rose 49°F (27°C) in just two minutes.

Also in South Dakota, Rapid City recorded a 49°F (27.2°C) temperature drop in just 15 minutes on January 10, 1911.

Strangest

We've all heard the expression, "It's raining cats and dogs." Well, on June 16, 1939, in Trowbridge, England, it actually "rained" tiny frogs. Strong winds had picked them up from nearby ponds, and they fell back to earth with the rain.

Wettest

Although Mt. Waialeale on the island of Kauai in Hawaii has one of the highest yearly average rainfalls at 460 inches (1,168 cm) a year, the actual highest yearly average now goes to Mawsynram, India, with 467.4 inches (1,187 cm). Cherrapunji, India, holds the record for any one year. Cherrapunji is affected by the monsoon, so it receives much summer rainfall and little in the winter. During a one-year period in 1860 to 1861, it rained a whopping 1,042 inches (2,647 cm)!

The largest recorded amount of rain to fall in one day was 71.9 inches (183 cm) at Foc-Foc, Réunion, an island in the Indian Ocean just west of Madagascar, on January 7 and 8, 1966, during tropical cyclone Denise. In the United States, Alvin, Texas, received 43 inches (109 cm) of rain in one day. That is more rain than most places in North America receive all year.

Although controversial, the highest rainfall in one hour in the United States is believed to be 13.80 inches (30 cm) in central West Virginia, recorded between 11:30 p.m. and 12:30 a.m. the night of August 4–5, 1943.

03 | Water in the Atmosphere

Have you ever wondered where all the water for rain and snow comes from? About half of it comes from plants, wet ground, rivers, and lakes. You may be surprised to know the other half of our precipitation on land is evaporated from the ocean. The ocean covers about 70 percent of the earth — a lot of surface for evaporation to take place.

Evaporation occurs any time water is exposed to air. Leave a glass of water out overnight, and the next morning a small amount of the water will be gone. A better example of evaporation is when you take a hot shower. As warm water droplets spray into the cooler air, water evaporates from them. When the air in the room becomes filled with water vapor it forms clouds. This water then condenses on the cold mirrors and windows. When the condensation becomes heavy enough, it gathers into drops and runs down the glass. What happens in your bathroom is similar to how water drops evaporate and condense to form clouds and rain.

Words to Know

cirrus clouds	relative humidity
cold front	stratus clouds
convection clouds	thunderstorm
evaporation	warm front
fog	water vapor
humid	

Level 1	Level 2	Level 3

The Global Water Cycle

In God's plan of creation, He set up scientific processes that sustain His creation. These processes include the global water cycle.

Evaporated ocean water is constantly being replaced by rainwater returning from the land by rivers and streams. This is called the water cycle or hydrological cycle. The cycle begins as vapor-laden air blows from the oceans to the land. The rain and snow fall on the land. Some of this precipitation is re-evaporated into the air. Rainwater that is not absorbed by the soil will run off into streams and rivers. Eventually, the water empties once again into the ocean. If we could follow one water molecule, it would make a circle from the ocean to the land and then back to the ocean.

Rainwater that does not run toward the ocean soaks deep into the ground. This water feeds what we call the aquifer or water table. When the water table is abundantly supplied, it is high enough to provide water for wells and springs. Where the water table is deep in the ground, the land is dry.

Condensation

Evaporation

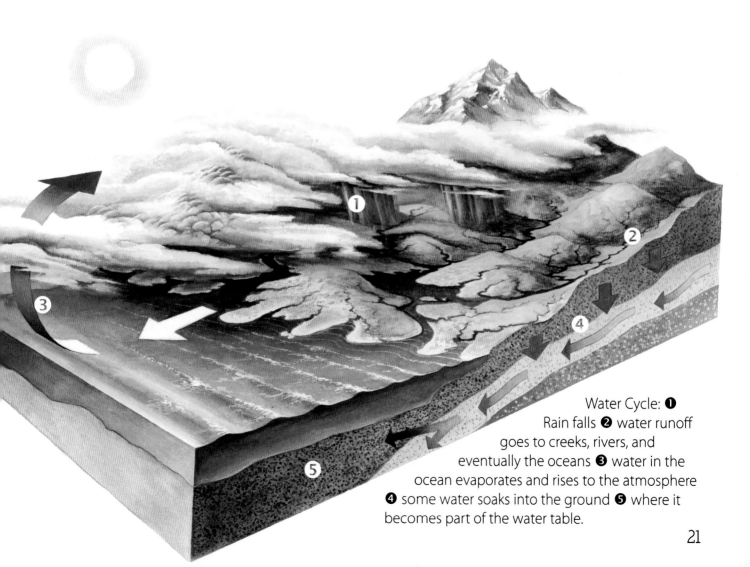

Water Cycle: ❶ Rain falls ❷ water runoff goes to creeks, rivers, and eventually the oceans ❸ water in the ocean evaporates and rises to the atmosphere ❹ some water soaks into the ground ❺ where it becomes part of the water table.

Runoff Essential for Food Chain

Runoff from rainstorms picks up chemicals from the soil and carry them to the ocean. Small amounts of carbon, iron, phosphorus, nitrogen, and other chemicals are nutrients that sustain sea life. Microscopic marine plants and animals, called plankton, require these chemicals, along with photosynthesis (combining of chemical compounds aided by sunlight), to survive. Plankton is an essential food for many marine creatures and even for baleen whales (they have whalebone plates for filtering plankton instead of teeth).

Through the water cycle, God provides life-sustaining water for man, animals, and plants. The run-off from the land to the ocean provides the nutrients necessary for marine plankton. These plankton are the beginning of the ocean food chain. In this way, the ocean will continue to have plentiful amounts of fish.

Missing Salt in the Ocean

Salt is added to the oceans every year by rivers and streams during runoff from the land and other processes, which we can estimate. Salt is also removed from the ocean, mainly by the process of sea spray, droplets of seawater carried up into the atmosphere by wind. Since more salt is ending up in the oceans, the salt is building up.

By measuring the total amount of salt in the ocean and dividing by the amount the salt is building up, we can estimate the age of the oceans. It turns out that the ocean is only about 40 to 60 million years old, if we consider only the rate of input of salt, while secular scientists claim it is about 3 billion years old, 60 times as old! But when we include all the salt added to the ocean during Noah's Flood, the age of the ocean is more like thousands of years.[*]

---

[*] Reference: *Earth's Catastrophic Past, Vol. 2,* Dr. Andrew Snelling, (Green Forest, AR: Master Books, 2014) page 879-881

Clouds

The atmosphere always contains a little bit of invisible water vapor. Clouds form when the atmosphere can no longer hold all of the invisible water vapor. This happens when the air has reached 100 percent relative humidity. At this point, any extra water vapor condenses into very small water drops that float in the air, just like what happens in your bathroom when you take a shower. Warm air holds more water vapor than cool air. So if warm, moist air is cooled, it will form a cloud.

Four Ways to Form Clouds

There are four different ways that moist air can be cooled enough to form clouds. It can be cooled by the ground at night from infrared radiation. This generates fog, which is really just a cloud on the ground that never rose.

Mountain clouds are formed when wind forces the air up a mountain ridge to where the air is cooler, and water vapor condenses.

Convection clouds occur when solar radiation heats up the earth's surface and the heated air rises. As the warm air rises and cools, any water vapor condenses to form clouds.

Frontal clouds form when the wind blows warmer moist air into cooler air or cooler air into warmer air. The collision of warmer and cooler air forms clouds.

Three Types of Clouds

Cumulus

Cumulus clouds are the white puffy clouds that look like cauliflower. Usually you see these fluffy white clouds on a bright, sunny day. They have flat bottoms, but the tops are always changing shape. A cumulus cloud means that the air is well mixed by up and down currents. When a cumulus cloud grows into a thunderstorm, the cloud is called a cumulonimbus cloud. This is a sign that the air is rising to near the stratosphere.

Stratus

Stratus clouds are low-altitude gray clouds that form a rather flat base. The name comes from the Latin word *stratus*, which means to stretch or extend. You will see the best stratus clouds as thick cloud blankets near the ocean. They are occasionally called "high fogs." Light rain and drizzle often fall from stratus clouds. When precipitation falls from stratus clouds, they are usually called nimbostratus.

Cirrus

Cirrus (sear-us) clouds are high-altitude clouds that often form as high as 35,000 feet (over 10 km) and often look thin and feathery. They are composed of ice crystals instead of water drops. This is because the upper atmosphere is around -50°F (-45°C), even if it is warm on the ground. Thin cirrus clouds are sometimes called "mares' tails" because they can look like the tails of a horse. These are the first clouds you see when a warm front is approaching.

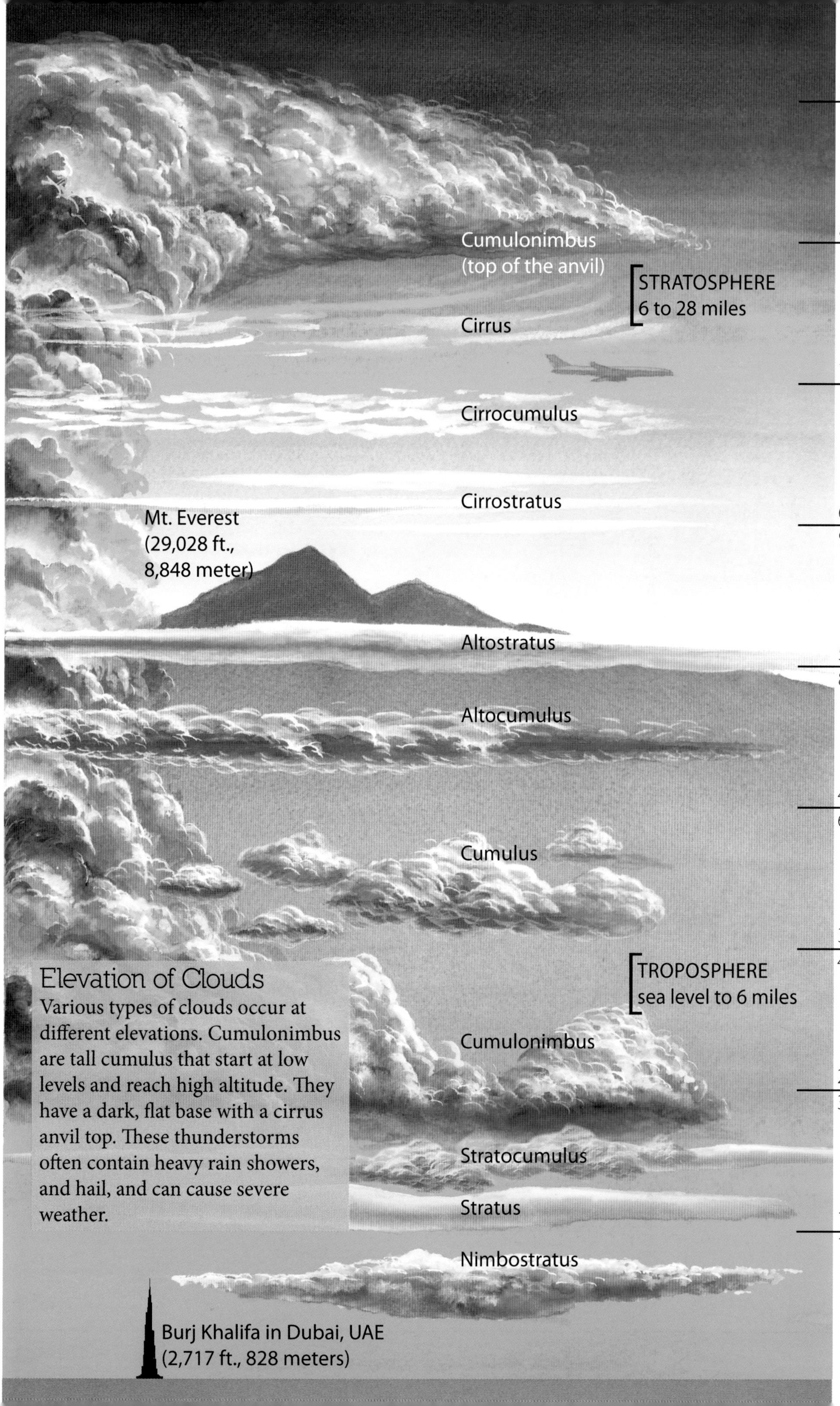

9 miles
14.4 km

Cumulonimbus
(top of the anvil)

8 miles
1.8 km

STRATOSPHERE
6 to 28 miles

Cirrus

7 miles
11.2 km

Cirrocumulus

Cirrostratus

6 miles
9.6 km

Mt. Everest
(29,028 ft.,
8,848 meter)

Altostratus

5 miles
8.0 km

Altocumulus

4 miles
6.4 km

Cumulus

3 miles
4.8 km

Elevation of Clouds

Various types of clouds occur at
different elevations. Cumulonimbus
are tall cumulus that start at low
levels and reach high altitude. They
have a dark, flat base with a cirrus
anvil top. These thunderstorms
often contain heavy rain showers,
and hail, and can cause severe
weather.

TROPOSPHERE
sea level to 6 miles

Cumulonimbus

2 miles
3.2 km

Stratocumulus

Stratus

1 mile
1.6 km

Nimbostratus

Burj Khalifa in Dubai, UAE
(2,717 ft., 828 meters)

Cloud Classification

In 1803, an English pharmacist, Luke Howard, devised a system to put clouds into ten distinct categories, depending upon the type of cloud and its elevation. His system proved so reliable that meteorologists are still using it today.

root	translations	level	form	main types
Cirro– or Cirrus–	curly, high	HIGH-LEVEL 20,000 feet and up (6,069 meters)	made of ice crystals	cirrus cirrostratus cirrocumulus
Alto–	mid (meaning high in Italian)	MID-LEVEL 6,000 – 20,000 feet (1,829 – 6,069 meters)	made up of water drops and ice crystals	altostratus altocumulus
Strato–	layer	LOW-LEVEL ground to 6,000 feet (ground – 1,829 meters)	made of water drops	Stratus
Cumulo–	heap			Cumulus
Nimbo–	rain, precipitation			

Cirrostratus

Cirrostratus are high cirrus clouds that have spread into a thin, milky sheet. Often the light shining through the ice crystals in the cloud forms a bright ring or halo around the sun or moon.

Cirrocumulus

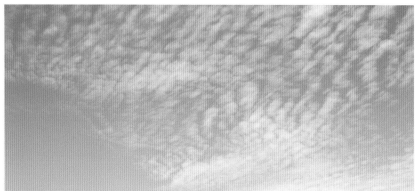

Cirrocumulus are tiny, high-altitude clumps of shadowless cirrus clouds. They often form waves and ripples and are called a mackerel sky because they resemble the scales of a fish.

Altostratus

Altostratus (above cumulus) is a thin sheet of clouds at medium heights that often cover the sky, making the sun look like it is shining through a frosted window.

Altocumulus

Altocumulus are puffs and rolls of clouds at medium heights and often have dark shadows.

Lenticular

Lenticular (lens-shaped) clouds are one type of altocumulus clouds. They are formed by waves in moderate-to-strong winds on the leeward side of mountains (away from the wind).

Nimbostratus

Nimbostratus are low gray stratus clouds with rain.

Stratocumulus

Stratocumulus are cumulus clouds that have spread horizontally to form broad sheets.

Warm Front

God has provided several processes to cause water vapor in the atmosphere to condense into clouds. A warm front is one of these processes. A warm front is that part of the low-pressure system in which warmer air pushes the colder air back.

Warm fronts in the Northern Hemisphere mostly move from the south or west. Warm air is less dense than cold air. As warm air pushes against cold air, the warmer air rises above the colder air.

Most clouds and precipitation are formed in areas of rising air in the atmosphere. As the air rises, it cools, but the amount of water vapor remains fixed. Finally, the temperature cools to the point where water vapor condenses to form clouds. We see the same effect on a clear night when there is plenty of water vapor in the air. As the temperature falls, the water vapor condenses on objects such as cars and grass. Clouds form the same way. As the clouds continue to rise, the water droplets grow larger until they become heavy enough for gravity to pull them to the ground. The warm front causes the air to rise at an angle, and the rising air produces rain and snow.

We can tell when a warm front is approaching by the type of clouds observed. Because the warm front slants, the first clouds we see will be high clouds. As the warm front comes closer, the clouds become thicker and lower. Finally, close to the warm front the clouds are low, and precipitation falls. After the warm front passes, the clouds usually decrease, and the precipitation stops.

Since most warm fronts move from west to east, sailors, farmers, and other people who depend upon the weather noticed the repeating pattern of clouds and precipitation. That is why they coined the weather saying: "Red skies at night, sailor's delight; red sky in the morning, sailor's warning." They learned that a red sunrise means a warm front was approaching from the west, bringing a beautiful sunrise. A brilliant sunset in the evening meant that the warm front had passed to the east.

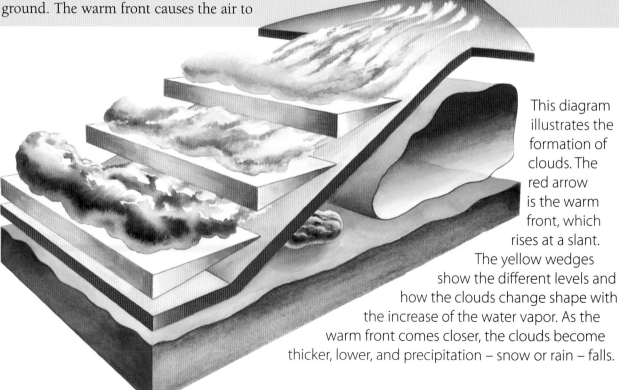

This diagram illustrates the formation of clouds. The red arrow is the warm front, which rises at a slant. The yellow wedges show the different levels and how the clouds change shape with the increase of the water vapor. As the warm front comes closer, the clouds become thicker, lower, and precipitation – snow or rain – falls.

Cold Front

God provided a second process in low-pressure systems that cause rain and snow. This is a cold front, in which cold air replaces warm air. Since the cold air is usually north and northwest of a low-pressure center, cold fronts most often come from the north or west. The colder air, being denser, dives underneath the warmer air. The less dense, warmer air is forced upward at a sharp angle. This rising air condenses and forms rain or snow.

Usually, the cold wind pushing the cold front from behind is much stronger than in warm fronts. Thus, cold fronts generally move faster than sluggish warm fronts. The fast motion causes the air to rise faster. In the warm season, rapidly rising air causes thunderstorms with cold

fronts. After the cold front passes, light rain or snow showers are left behind. When the cold front is well past, the skies usually clear.

If a faster-moving cold front catches up to a warm front, it is called an occluded front. It is represented on a weather map by alternating triangles and semicircles pointing in the direction of movement. Occluded fronts act a lot like cold fronts.

The most dreaded type of cold front is the Alberta Clipper in the central and eastern United States. This is an Arctic cold front in which cold Alaskan or Canadian air sweeps south or southeast into the United States as a low-pressure center passes to the east. Sometimes the weather can change from mild to below zero in a matter of several hours. Temperature drops of more than 70°F (40°C) can occur within 24 hours. It is called an Alberta Clipper because these cold fronts usually start in Alberta, Canada.

The dynamics of rain forming in a cold front. Notice the cold air slips under the warmer air, forcing it higher until it produces precipitation.

Temperature 80° F
Humidity 60%
Dew Point 65° F

The Dew Point

As air cools, it is able to hold less and less invisible water vapor. When the air can no longer hold any more vapor (point of saturation), it has reached its dew point temperature. Moisture in the air then condenses to form clouds or fog. Even before the water vapor reaches the dew point, it condenses into droplets when it comes into contact with a cold surface.

Fog

Fog is essentially a cloud that forms on the ground. Fog can form in several ways. The most common way is on a clear night when the temperature drops, and the relative humidity rises to 100 percent. At this point, the temperature has dropped to the dew point temperature, and the water vapor in the air has to condense out as liquid drops. This type of fog is most common during the wintertime in many mountain valleys of the world. It can occur over the central and eastern United States most of the year. These areas can be quite moist, even in the summer, so it does

not take much of a temperature drop at night to form fog.

Fog can form over water, usually at night. Evaporation into the air moistens the air until fog forms. This is called evaporation fog. In this case, the increase in water vapor in the air raises the dew point temperature and the relative humidity. So it is easier for the temperature to fall to the dew point temperature, or maybe the dew point temperature will rise up to the air temperature.

Conditions that create fog

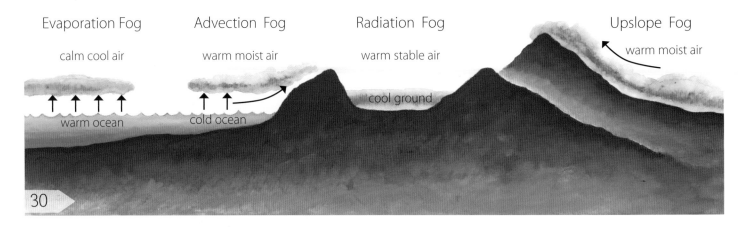

Evaporation Fog
calm cool air
warm ocean

Advection Fog
warm moist air
cold ocean

Radiation Fog
warm stable air
cool ground

Upslope Fog
warm moist air

The National Weather Service will issue a Dense Fog Advisory for periods of thick fog that limits visibility to below one quarter of a mile for at least a two-hour period.

Another way for fog to form is for moist air to blow into cool air. In this way, the cool air moistens up and the relative humidity increases until fog forms.

A third mechanism that forms fog occurs in mountainous or hilly terrain. Fog will occur when low clouds intersect the ground when trying to pass over high terrain. Sometimes fog will form even if moist air is uplifted over mountains. The clouds can form near the higher parts of the mountains. If you were up that high, it would be fog to you.

In the western United States during winter, an inversion is usually present in many of the mountain valleys. An inversion is where the temperature near the surface of the ground is colder than the air above it. If a stationary high-pressure system is over the area, the fog can persist under the inversion for days. This is why fog can sometimes last for weeks in the San Joaquin and Sacramento Valleys of California. The fog in these valleys is called "Tule fog." It usually disperses when a low-pressure system moves into the area or after a cold front passes through.

04 | Thunderstorms

A beautiful summer sun disappears as a line of dark clouds approach. You've heard distant rumbling for a while and watched as the wind blew the storm in your direction. Soon thunder crashes and jagged bolts of lightning pierce the sky. You run for cover just before the downpour hits.

After a dramatic drum roll, clouds heavy with water release their payload. Rain pelts down in huge drops, depositing as much as one hundred million gallons of water within an hour. It comes so quickly that much of it runs off into gutters beside the road. In the country, it rushes through gullies and into swelling streams. The storm lasts only an hour or so; then the sun bursts forth. The summer thunderstorm moves on, leaving the earth smelling moist and fresh once again.

Words to Know

downdraft	static electricity
electricity	updraft
electrons	latent heat

| Level 1 | Level 2 | Level 3 |

How Many Thunderstorms?

At any one moment, about 1,800 thunderstorms occur around the earth. Each year, there are 16 million thunderstorms. Approximately one hundred thousand of these thunderstorms take place annually in the United States. Most of the storms in the United States occur in the southeast.

Most of the world's thunderstorms occur in the tropics. For example, central Africa and Indonesia have storms nearly every day. Imagine living in Kampala, Uganda, where thunderstorms strike on 242 days each year! Kampala is believed by experts to hold the world's record for thunderstorms in a year.

A thunderstorm releases an immense amount of electrical power in a small area of about one hundred square miles. In only 20 minutes, power from one thunderstorm can produce a week's worth of electricity for a large city. Across the earth, 40 to 50 lightning bolts strike every second. That adds up to 1.4 billion flashes per year worldwide.

The Formation of Thunderstorms

Thunderstorms develop from fluffy cumulus clouds. A gentle cumulus cloud can suddenly mushroom into a giant thunderstorm — a cumulonimbus cloud. Three conditions are necessary to make this dramatic change. The first is a large difference in temperature between the ground and upper troposphere. The second requirement is plenty of moisture in the lower atmosphere. The third condition is a trigger — a process to start the thunderstorm. Once such a storm is triggered, the moisture and temperature differences cause strong winds to blow upward from the ground. These winds are called updrafts.

Usually there are more clouds in the afternoon than in the early morning. This is because the ground has warmed up enough by the afternoon for updrafts to develop. If there is very little moisture, an updraft has to go much higher before the water vapor condenses into a cloud. Sometimes the air will rise as high as 5,000 to 10,000 feet (1,524 to 3,048 m) above the ground before a little cumulus cloud condenses from the invisible water vapor.

The Life Cycle of a Thunderstorm

High, puffy little clouds do not change until a large amount of moisture is added. This moisture strengthens the updraft. Moisture adds heat, called latent heat, which means the cloud will warm inside and rise even faster. Latent heat is the heat it takes to evaporate water, which is released upon condensation in the cloud. The moisture and extra heating causes the cumulus cloud to mushroom upward and transform into a huge towering cumulus or cumulonimbus. The winds inside this cloud can be very strong. Sometimes the updraft will reach 60 mph (96 kph). As the air and moisture in the cloud rises, it continually cools upward because of expansion in the lower pressure of the upper troposphere.

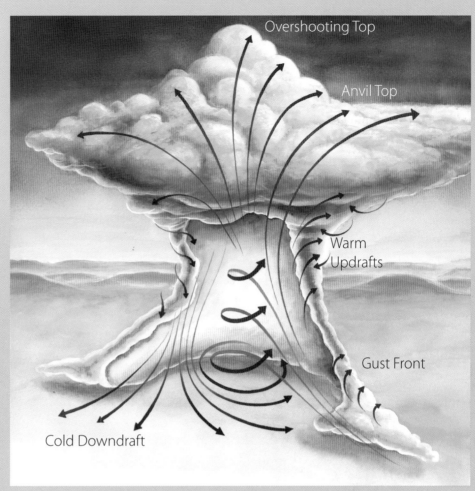

The Anatomy of a Thunderstorm

Thunder and lightning usually start when the top of the cloud reaches about 25,000 feet (7,620 m). The inside of the cloud by this time is cold enough that the water drops are turned into ice crystals.

A cumulus cloud slows down and eventually stops growing when it hits the stratosphere, a warmer layer of air in the upper atmosphere. Some thunderstorms grow twice as high as Mount Everest. Strong upper winds in the upper troposphere and stratosphere brush off the top of the cloud and spread it. This makes the cloud resemble the top of a mushroom or an anvil. An anvil is a block of metal a blacksmith hammers against when shaping horseshoes. The ice crystals in the anvil cloud give it a fuzzy look.

As a thunderstorm develops, water drops or ice crystals inside the cloud grow by colliding and merging with each other. The bottom of the cloud grows dark with water waiting to fall. When the drops become so heavy that the updraft inside the cloud cannot sweep them up anymore, they fall by gravity from the cloud as rain or hail. Even as they fall, the water drops grow by combining with the smaller drops. This produces huge splashing raindrops. Hail gains its size inside the cloud. The falling hail and raindrops start a downdraft that eventually interferes with the moist updraft and weakens the thunderstorm. One thunderstorm cloud usually runs out of energy within 30 to 50 minutes.

Usually, thunderstorms come in a large group. One marches behind the other. So, as one thunderstorm weakens in the group, another grows. Because the ground usually cools off at night, thunderstorms normally don't last past sunset. Sometimes, though, the ground temperature remains warm all night. On a hot summer evening, the storms continue on into the night until the ground cools. Also, if a low-pressure system is in the area, thunderstorms can occur at night.

A Blessing

Overall, thunderstorms are a great blessing to man and all living creatures. They are the main source of water for the interior of mid-latitude continents during the summer. Plants receive an abundance of life-sustaining rainfall when they need it the most. Without the thunderstorms, these continents would become parched and dry. Fish would die, crops would fail, and animals would perish. Thunderstorms provide water for most of the world's food.

Thunderstorms provide other benefits we often take for granted. They are natural air conditioners. Heated air at the surface rises upward into the high atmosphere where the heat is released into space. Cloud formation provides shade. Rain and hail bring refreshing cooling after a hot day. Thunderstorms act collectively like a thermostat to keep the earth as a whole from becoming too hot. Without this upward heat pump, the earth would be as much as 20°F (11°C) warmer.

Thunderstorms also are one of God's air cleaners. During the summer, dust, haze, and other pollutants collect in the lower atmosphere. Rising air, either in cumulus clouds or in thunderstorms, spreads the pollution higher in the atmosphere where it is dispersed. Rain from thunderstorms washes many of these particles out of the air.

Lightning in thunderstorms serves a purpose as well. It helps maintain the electrical balance of the earth and atmosphere. Lightning also forms fertilizer. When it splits the sky, lightning changes nitrogen gas in the air into nitrogen compounds. These, in turn, fall to the earth and are added to the soil. Nitrogen is one of the main ingredients in fertilizer. Ten percent of the nitrogen fertilizer needed for farming is provided by lightning.

So, despite the dangers of lightning, thunderstorms are a blessing to us. They provide summer water, cool the earth, and clean the air. Lightning balances the earth's electricity and helps fertilize the soil. Lightning and thunderstorms are part of God's plan for sustaining life on earth. Rainbows sometimes are seen with thunderstorms. The sun shines through drops of falling rain, causing the light to split into a spectrum of colors. This is a reminder of God's promise never to flood the whole earth again as He did at the time of Noah.

Lightning Is Electricity

You might have wondered what causes lightning, a strong electrical discharge. In 1772, Benjamin Franklin was the first to demonstrate that a thunderstorm generates electricity. Lightning is like the static electricity you experience when you rub your foot on a rug and touch a doorknob. Your foot rubs electrons from the rug that travel through you to your fingertips. A spark of electricity shoots from your finger to the doorknob. In a thunderstorm, the lower cloud becomes charged with as much as 100 million volts of electricity. This electricity is discharged either within the cloud, to the ground, to another cloud, or even into the air. Lightning has even been known to travel from the ground upward to the cloud. In 1993, scientists discovered lightning bolts that shot upward from the top of a cumulonimbus cloud.

Lightning SAFETY TIPS

Lightning is dangerous, and there are safety rules you should know during a thunderstorm.

- If lightning approaches, seek shelter in a house, car, or low area, but not in a shed. Inside the house, do not use the telephone or any appliance. Do not bathe or take a shower.

- Stay away from water.

- Do not stand on a hilltop. Avoid being the tallest object.

- Do not seek shelter under an isolated tree.

- Stay away from metal pipes, fences, and wire clotheslines.

- If your hair stands on end while outside, immediately drop to the ground and curl into a ball.

Electrical charges build up in the cloud. Positive (+) at the top, and negative (-) at the bottom.

Leader stroke discharges the negative charge in the cloud into the positively charged ground.

Return stroke flashes up from the ground, heating the air. The air expands with a clap of thunder.

Origin of Lightning and Thunder

Scientists are still trying to understand lightning. Many scientists think that lightning is formed when electricity builds up in the cloud as a result of ice particles colliding. Negative electrons rub off onto larger ice particles. These crystals are so heavy they descend to the lower part of the cloud. The smaller ice crystals become positively charged and rise to the top of the clouds in the powerful updrafts. This process separates the negative charges from the positive charges. This separation causes a large difference in voltage between the bottom and the top of the cloud, and between the ground and the cloud bottom. Since opposite charges attract, the voltage difference becomes so large that a massive spark pierces the air. The electrons shoot to the area of the positive charge, either to the ground or up into the cloud or even into the air or to another cloud.

There are many problems with this theory, however. Scientists have shown that even small cumulus clouds can generate electricity. They have also found that electricity can form without ice crystals. Sometimes, high amounts of electricity flow from the air into the cloud. Since, in most cases, the bottom of the cloud is negatively charged with electrons, cloud to ground lightning usually is negatively charged. But, 2 to 3 percent of these lightning bolts are not negative electrons, but positive charges. The positively charged bolts are the most dangerous. Scientists cannot explain how lighting is positively charged. Nature is very complex, and there is still much we need to learn about it.

Fast cameras have shown the process of lightning better. As the bottom of the cloud becomes more negatively charged with

the ground positive, an invisible "leader" or channel of ionized air progresses from the bottom of the cloud to the ground. Upon reaching the ground, the lightning bolt races to the ground. In fact, many bolts race to the ground in quick succession.

Thunder is created when a lightning bolt splits the air. It heats the surrounding air molecules to 50,000°F (28,000°C) within a few millionths of a second. That is five times the temperature of the sun's surface. This explosive temperature rise next to the large spark causes the air to expand violently. This expansion generates thunder. Sound is caused by vibrations or waves in the air that your ear picks up. A way to demonstrate sound is to feel the vibrations of a lower sound played through a "subwoofer" speaker. It makes the room rumble.

Echoes

Sound echoes and, therefore, you hear it differently when it is close rather than when it is far away. When lightning is near, it sounds like a sharp crack. But when it is farther away, it makes a rumbling noise. The rumble is caused by sound waves bouncing off objects, forming echoes

Distance

You might think thunder and lightning happen at the same time since the sound waves explode at the same time as the lightning bolts. But they don't. Thunder travels at the speed of sound, which is 750 mph (1,200 kph). Lightning travels at the speed of light, a million times faster than the speed of sound. You can calculate how many miles the thunderstorm is from you by counting the number of seconds between the lightning and the thunder. Then divide the seconds by five. Thunder normally can be heard up to seven miles (11 km) away. On a quiet day, a person might hear a faint rumble from 20 miles (32 km) away.

05 | Dangerous Thunderstorms

Although most thunderstorms just bring brief heavy rain and moderate winds, some are ferocious. Of the 100,000 thunderstorms that occur in the United States each year, one out of ten brings damaging winds, large hail, tornadoes, and flash floods. These often injure and kill people and destroy crops and homes.

People often wonder why a God as wonderful as ours would allow dangerous thunderstorms. There is no simple answer for each event, especially if someone is badly hurt. But the Bible says that all nature groans for God's redemption. Nature is a little out of whack as the result of sin, after Adam and Eve rebelled against God. Yet even dangerous storms can give us a hint of God's power. God gives mankind the knowledge and ability to predict dangerous weather patterns so we can protect ourselves. This is one of His provisions for us.

Words to Know

flash flood	supercooled drops
hailstones	funnel cloud
supercell	microburst
tornado	waterspout,
dust devil	tornado alley

Level 1	Level 2	Level 3

What Causes Severe Thunderstorms

Regular thunderstorms develop when warm air near the ground combines with moist air, causing an updraft. A severe thunderstorm requires both a strong updraft and a strong downdraft. A strong updraft is formed under three conditions:

❶ when the ground is extra warm,

❷ the air is extra moist, and

❸ the air above is extra cool.

The stronger the updraft, the more violent the thunderstorm.

When large raindrops or hail form in the strong updraft, they produce a strong downdraft as they fall. Severe thunderstorm downdrafts become even stronger when there is dry air 6,000 to 12,000 feet (2 to 4 km) above the ground.

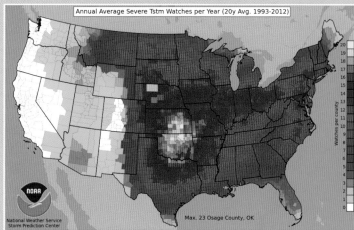

Many countries experience severe thunderstorms. However, the United States experiences the most severe thunderstorms because of its geography. During spring and summer in the United States, extra moist air blows northward from the Gulf of Mexico over the well-heated plains. The extra moisture comes from the warm water of the Gulf of Mexico. Warm water evaporates more quickly than cold water, and warm air holds more water vapor than cool air. The combination of warm earth and moist air creates thunderstorms. This powerful combination generates the severe thunderstorms in the United States. Most of these occur in the southern and central Midwest. This area stretches from Texas and Oklahoma north into Kansas and Nebraska and east into Arkansas and Missouri. Because the Gulf of Mexico's moisture moves east, the eastern United States has more severe thunderstorms than west of the Rockies or the northern Midwest.

Flash Floods

Flash floods occur when slow-moving thunderstorms drop an unusual amount of water on a small area. A flash flood is a rapid rise in the level of the water; it does not mean a wall of water is approaching. It rains so hard the water cannot soak into the ground. The longer it rains, the greater the chance of a flash flood, and the more severe the flood will become. The water rushes down the mountainsides or hills into the streams and rivers. These streams and rivers cannot carry all the water, so it quickly floods. The most severe flash floods cause the water levels to rise rapidly to dangerous levels in streams, dry washes, or canyons. They can also trigger catastrophic mud slides. Flash floods move at rapid speeds, up to about 20 to 30 mph down a steep canyon, and have been known to roll big boulders, tear out trees, and destroy buildings and bridges.

Flash floods also occur when two or more gully-washing thunderstorms hit the same spot, one right after the other. They can occur when a dam bursts or an ice or debris jam breaks up, causing a rush of water to roar downstream. Flash floods can also happen when it rains heavily on rapidly melting snow.

If thunderstorms are in the area, stay out of low places like gullies or stream beds. Cars should not be driven through water that is flowing over a road or bridge. Shallow, swiftly flowing water can wash a car off the roadway. It only takes two feet of water to float most cars. Worse yet, the road under the water may already have been washed out, leaving a deep hole. A flash flood can easily overturn a car, van, or recreational vehicle and trap its occupants. If your car stalls in flood waters, you must get out as fast as possible and go to higher ground. Nearly half the people who die in flash floods in the United States die in automobiles.

Hail and Wind Damage

Have you ever seen hail the size of a golf ball? You may have, especially if you live in the Midwest of the United States. For a thunderstorm to be considered severe, the hail needs to be only ¾ inch (1.9 cm) in diameter, the size of a dime. About 5,000 hailstorms a year in the United States produce hail ¾ of an inch or larger.

Hail does a tremendous amount of damage every year. Hail damage occurs in swaths, up to a few miles wide and hundreds of miles long. It causes about 2 billion dollars in crop losses in North America alone each year. Even small hail with strong winds can mow down a field of wheat within minutes. Hail can severely dent cars, roofs, and siding. It sometimes breaks windows. Large hailstones can injure and sometimes kill small animals.

Because of crop damage, there have been many interesting experiments to suppress hail. Back in the 16th century, farmers used to shoot cannons at thunderstorms thinking this would destroy the hail. Cloud seeding (attempts to start rainfall by distributing dry ice crystals or silver iodide smoke through clouds) is the more modern method, but it is expensive, and it is difficult to know how well the method works.

Severe thunderstorms also cause wind damage. For a thunderstorm to be considered severe in the United States, it has to produce winds of 58 mph (93 kph) or greater. The wind speed rule may vary a little in other countries, but essentially is the lowest wind speed that begins to cause damage. The wind in some severe thunderstorms, however, can gust to more than 100 mph (160 kph). Winds this powerful can

cause a huge amount of damage. They can tear roofs off houses or even blow them over. Mobile homes can be flattened by strong winds in severe thunderstorms. If the ground is dry, the strong wind ahead of a severe thunderstorm causes a dust storm.

A record-setting hailstone that fell in Vivian, South Dakota on July 23, 2010. The hailstone broke the United States record for the largest hailstone. It was 8 in. (20.32 cm) in diameter and weighted 1 lb. 15 oz. (869 grams).

The Formation of Hail

Hail forms as water freezes within up and down drafts within a thunderstorm. The stronger the updraft in the cumulonimbus cloud, the larger the hail. The stronger updrafts take the cumulonimbus cloud so high that the water drop has to travel very far before it reaches the top of the cloud. The farther is has to travel up and then down, the more opportunities it has to join with other supercooled drops. It takes ten billion cloud droplets to form a golf ball-sized hailstone.

The United States and world records for the largest hailstone have been set several times since about 1970. It is uncertain what the world record is. Although there have been reports of even larger hailstones, the official world record is 8.0 inches (20 cm) in diameter that fell on Vivian, South Dakota, on July 23, 2010. The largest circumference ever documented in the world was from a hailstone collected in Aurora in south-central Nebraska on June 22, 2003. It is seven inches (17.8 cm) wide and had a circumference of 18.75 inches (47.6 cm). The old record for the United States occurred at Coffeyville, Kansas, on September 3, 1970. It weighed 1.67 pounds (0.75 kg) and was 5.5 inches (14 cm) across.

Hailstones are made of alternating rings of clear and cloudy ice. The rings represent different rates of freezing on the hailstone. The cloudy ice is caused mainly by rapid freezing, trapping many small air bubbles. The clear ring is caused by slow freezing of the water, which allows the bubbles to escape. Hail is mostly round, but sometimes it comes in strange shapes. Some hailstones have ragged edges, or ice spikes, like quartz crystals.

Hail normally lasts only a few minutes. But on June 3, 1959, a hailstorm in Seldon, Kansas, lasted 85 minutes and covered the town 18 inches deep over a 54 square mile (117 square km) area. Sometimes the wind blows hail into drifts up to three feet deep. Hail accompanied by heavy rainfall blocked a culvert in a draw in Clayton, New Mexico, on August 13, 2004. The clogged stream caused hail to pile up 15 feet (4.6 m) deep! At other times, hail falls with no wind.

Hail forms in the strong wind currents of cumulonimbus clouds.

Hail and Strong Winds in More Depth

A hailstone begins as an innocent little water drop or a round snow pellet in a cloud. The drop has already grown by collecting a million cloud droplets. The little drop is blown by a strong updraft inside the cloud to where it meets with some supercooled water drops. These supercooled drops are still liquid water even though the temperature is below freezing, which can happen with quick freezing in the air. When the little drop collides with these supercooled drops, they join company. The little drop has now become a hailstone.

The little hailstone is tossed up inside the cloud, continuing to collect supercooled drops. The hailstone gets larger and larger until it reaches the top of the cloud. Then it runs out of updraft and falls back down through the cloud. On the way down it gets even bigger as it bangs into more supercooled drops. It can go up and down a few more times. If it ends up in a very fast downdraft, it can hit the earth at up to 90 mph (144 kph), bouncing like popcorn. If the hailstone hits soil, it can bury itself.

It is fun to watch, but from under cover. Large hail can sting, bruise, or tear your skin. If it is extra big, your life could be in danger.

The strong winds are caused by two mechanisms. One is the strong downdraft from the thunderstorm hitting the ground and spreading out horizontally. The second mechanism is the evaporation of rain that causes the air to cool and have higher pressure. There is almost always lower pressure ahead of the thunderstorm. So the difference between the high pressure and low pressure, which is proportional to the strength of the wind, becomes stronger.

Severe thunderstorms bring such chaotic winds near the ground that it is dangerous for airplanes. Weathermen call these chaotic winds microbursts or wind shear. Microbursts have caused airplanes to crash while landing or taking off from airports. Many airports have installed instruments to detect the microbursts, so they can warn the pilots.

Microburst

Tornadoes

Some thunderstorms give birth to tornadoes. A tornado is a violently rotating, tall, narrow column of wind that makes contact with the ground. It is made visible by the condensation of water vapor and is surrounded by a cloud of flying debris and dust near the ground. The tornado has to touch the ground before it is officially called a tornado. A whirling cloud that does not touch the ground is called a funnel cloud.

Some people confuse hurricanes with tornadoes. Tornadoes are small, while hurricanes cover hundreds of miles or kilometers. However, tornadoes will sometimes form on the edge of hurricanes.

Dust devils are not tornadoes, although they whirl around, collecting dust and debris. Dust devils are formed on warm, sunny days above a dry field caused by local updrafts. They twist between 15 and 30 mph (30 to 50 kph) and extend only several hundred feet (around 100 m) above the ground. They are caused by superheated air just above the ground, resulting in spiraling updrafts.

When a tornado touches down on water, it is called a waterspout. Although waterspouts are normally weak, one can become stronger if it moves over land. A strong waterspout can sink a small boat. Waterspouts are most frequent in the Atlantic and Indian Oceans near the equator, in the Mediterranean Sea, and in the Gulf of Mexico. Research has shown that the largest number of waterspouts occur in the Florida Keys of the United States.

funnel cloud

dust devil

water spout

A summer storm gathers on the horizon

A supercell thunderstorm — notice the beautiful structure. Supercells are formed when factors that include strong speed, wind shear, and a height of at least 20,000 feet combine.

How Tornadoes Form

Although scientists do not know the exact mechanism that forms tornadoes, they now think they understand the life cycle of tornadoes. Tornadoes, especially the strong ones, often start within a type of a severe thunderstorm called a supercell, a horizontally rotating current of air a few miles up in the cloud that is 1 to 6 miles (1.6 to 10 km) in diameter. Then with increasing rainfall, the rain cools the air and causes a strong downdraft to form called the "rear flank downdraft." This downdraft picks up speed as it approaches the ground and drags the rotating supercell down toward the ground.

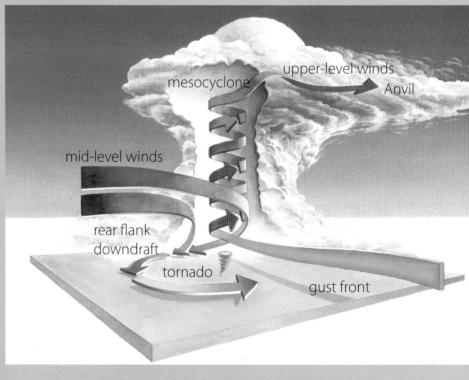

As the stretched rotation of the supercell reaches below the bottom of the cloud, it meets the strong updraft where the wall cloud forms. This focuses the supercell rotation into a funnel cloud that descends to the ground to form a tornado.

What scientists do not understand is how strong tornadoes can form without a supercell. Moreover, many supercells do not produce tornadoes. Scientists still do not understand how stretching of the supercell downward produces a narrow tornado. Predicting tornado intensity and longevity remains a challenge.

Storm Chasers

Most people run from tornadoes, but some scientists run toward them. These people are professional storm chasers. They try to get as close to the tornado as they can. They want to film them and learn more about them. This is not something you should try yourself unless you have a death wish. Some tornado chasers have been struck by lightning, bashed by large hailstones, sucked inside tornadoes, and killed.

Storm chasers have learned that a tornado forms in a special spot under the thunderstorm where there is little rain or lightning, in the southwest part of the storm cloud. A tornado

storm chasers

usually is found between the strong updraft and the downdraft. All strong tornadoes form in a low overhanging cloud that lies just below the thunderstorm. This is called a wall cloud.

Joplin, MO, tornado on May 21, 2011, devastates city, St. Johns Hospital in background

Tornado Watches and Warnings

A **tornado watch** is when conditions are favorable for the development of severe thunderstorms that are capable of producing tornadoes.

A **particularly dangerous situation** is a type of warning used often in combination with severe weather watches in order to highlight an especially serious or dangerous conditions for life-threatening weather — an outbreak of tornadoes or other extreme weather hazard.

Tornado warnings are issued when a tornado has been reported on the ground or funnel clouds

in the sky have been spotted or strong rotation is indicated by radar. Waterspouts preparing to make landfall is another time when a tornado warning is issued.

A **particularly dangerous situation tornado warning** is one where a tornado has been spotted or confirmed to be on the ground and it is expected to be a significant event.

A **tornado emergency** is often used in heavily populated areas where significant potential for damage or loss of life is possible.

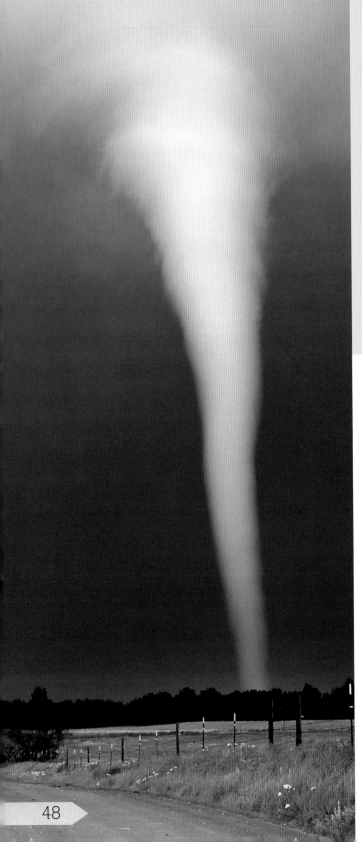

Tornadoes are a regular feature for many who live in states within the Great Plains region of the United States. They occur more frequently in the central parts of the U.S. between the Rocky Mountains and the Appalachian Mountains.

Tornado Types

Tornadoes vary in size and strength. They are classified by the Fujita or "F" scale, named after a famous atmospheric scientist. In 2007, the Fujita scale was changed to the enhanced Fujita scale, or "EF" scale to better reflect tornado damage. Like the F scale, the EF scale also varies from 0 to 5. Some look like thin ropes, and these would be F0 or F1 tornadoes. These are about a hundred feet across and spin at about 150 mph (240 kph). They are not considered very strong. They commonly touch down only a couple of minutes and then go back up into the cloud. This type of tornado moves at about 25 mph (40 kph). The damage path, mostly minor, is only about 150 feet (50 meters) wide and 1 mile (1/2 km) long.

The most dangerous tornadoes are the thick black spiraling clouds that may be 2,000 feet (700 meters) across or more. These spin at up to 250 to 300 mph (400 to 480 kph) and are F4 or F5 tornadoes. They can sweep across the land at up to 50 mph (80 kph). Strong tornadoes can move along the ground for 100 miles (160 km) and have a damage path of over a mile (1.6 km) wide.

Tornado SAFETY TIPS

- Go to the basement or the lowest floor of a house or building. Huddle close to the center of the house or building. Stay away from windows. Find a piece of strong furniture or a mattress to duck under or hide in a closet and wait until it is over.

- If you are in school when a tornado hits, an interior hallway on the lowest floor is safer than a classroom that has windows. Crouch near the wall. Bend over, placing your hands on the back of your head. By all means, stay out of auditoriums, gymnasiums, and other similar structures that have high ceilings.

- If you are in a mobile home or car, get out and seek shelter elsewhere.

- If you cannot find shelter, lie in a ditch or find the lowest, protected ground and cover your head with your hands.

These tips also apply for severe thunderstorms.

Path of Destruction

With as much as we know about tornadoes, there is still so much more to learn. In the aftermath of tragedies like the Moore or Joplin tornadoes, people ask why people are at risk or killed even though stronger construction methods and more warning systems are available. For areas prone to this type of violent weather, most people would be unable to afford a home that could stand up to 250+ mile per hour winds.

The 2013 Oklahoma City tornado as it passed through south part of the city.

A photograph giving an aerial view of tornado damage in Moore, OK, on May 21, 2013.

Many choose to have underground shelters, though not all communities or businesses have public shelters available. Basements are also used as shelters, but unless the roof of it is concrete, it becomes an area for debris to accumulate from the destroyed home (Moore, OK).

Rescue crews struggle with a mountain of debris while trying to find survivors, including schoolchildren and teachers from two Moore, OK, schools. Seven students were killed at the Plaza Towers Elementary School in addition to 17 other fatalities from the storm amidst over $2 billion in damage to the community.

Tornado Characteristics

Sometimes, a tornado is difficult to see. All that is visible is the top of the tornado and a small whirl of dust at the ground. These nearly invisible tornadoes fool many people. If you know what to look for, it won't trick you. A concentrated swirl of dust or debris near the ground gives it away. The tornado itself is invisible because water vapor inside the funnel has not yet condensed to form a cloud. Another reason is that not enough dirt and dust have been sucked up into the tornado to mark it.

Most people have heard of the terrible damage that tornadoes cause. Toppled buildings, rolled mobile homes, and uprooted trees are common due to the strong rotating winds. Sometimes they pick up debris that becomes deadly missiles. Tornadoes have even been known to drive a piece of straw into a wood beam. In 1975, a tornado in Mississippi picked up a home freezer and dropped it more than a mile away. Tornadoes passing over barnyards have even stripped chickens of their feathers.

EF4-rated tornado damage in Ringgold, GA. that occurred during the April 25–28, 2011 tornado outbreak.

One of the worst tornadoes occurred on April 26, 1989, 40 miles (60 km) north of Dhaka, Bangladesh. A nighttime tornado killed 1,109 people, injured 15,000, and left another 100,000 homeless.

The deadliest tornado recorded in the United States was the Tri-State Tornado on March 18, 1925. It developed in southeast Missouri, raced 60 mph (95 kph) through southern Illinois, and broke up in southeast Indiana in about 3 hours and 40 minutes. The city of DeSoto, Illinois, was completely destroyed. The tornado killed 689 people, injured 2,000, and left 11,000 homeless.

Sometimes the atmosphere is especially ripe for a large number of tornadoes in a small area. These are called tornado outbreaks. Among the worst in the United States happened on April 3 and 4, 1974. An amazing 148 tornadoes in just two days hit in a 13-state area of the Midwest! The cities of Xenia, Ohio, and Brandenburg, Kentucky, were almost completely destroyed. This outbreak killed 315 people, injured more than 6,000 and demolished over 9,600 homes.

Advances in the way that tornado warnings are issued and changes in the way tornadoes are rated due to the type of damage have also changed in the last 40 years. A tornado outbreak from April 25 till April 28, 2011 was one of the largest ever documented in the United States. With 355 tornadoes, 211 in a single 24-hour time frame, leaving 348 dead, this outbreak helped to increase the number of tornadoes in the month of April to almost three times as many as the 1974 record to a total of 765.

Fortunately, tornadoes are unusual, even in the midwestern United States. Some people live their entire lives in tornado alley and never see one. But if you see one heading for you, it can be very frightening. People who have been in or near a tornado report that it sounds like 1,000 freight trains roaring down on them. Despite the destruction caused by tornadoes in the United States, only an average of about 60 people a year are killed, mostly from flying debris. Property damage is usually in the hundreds of millions of dollars. Although the U.S. population has increased, the number of tornado deaths has gone down over the years. This is due to improved discovery and warning methods by the National Weather Service. It is expected more lives will be saved as warnings improve. However, property damage has skyrocketed upward.

Forecasting Tornadoes

Tornadoes are generally unpredictable. They often change shape as they move. They can lift off the ground, go back up into the cloud, and touch down again a short distance away. Just because a tornado has gone back up into a cloud does not mean the danger is over. It can return from the same thunderstorm, or a new tornado can come from a nearby thunderstorm.

Tornado forecasting is the ultimate challenge for a weather forecaster because lives and property are at stake. A tornado watch is issued for large areas when atmospheric conditions seem right for tornadoes, but none have occurred yet. A tornado warning is issued when a tornado or funnel cloud is sighted or seen on radar. Funnel clouds often drop to the ground and become tornadoes.

A special type of radar, called Doppler radar, is used in weather offices across the United States. They have the unique ability to detect wind speed and direction inside a dangerous thunderstorm. With the new radar, weathermen can see the supercell whirling inside the cloud up to 20 minutes before a tornado touches the ground. This radar is especially helpful in tornado alley because it gives people enough time to find a safe place. If a big tornado is close to the Doppler radar, it can even show up on the screen.

Doppler radar map

June 24, 2003. Minutes before, the F4 tornado destroyed the village of Manchester, South Dakota.

06 | Hurricanes

Most people think of the tropics as mostly sunny and hot. The tropics are the area of the earth from 30° above to 30° below the equator. The tropical zone looks like a belt wrapped around the stomach of the world. However, large sections of the tropics are rainy and mild most of the year.

What is the difference between hurricanes, cyclones, and typhoon? Basically, just their locations. They are all the same kind of weather phenomenon. In the South Pacific and Indian Ocean, they are known as cyclones. Typhoon is the word used to describe this weather event in the Northwest Pacific. In the Atlantic and Northeast Pacific, the word to describe them is hurricane.

Words to Know

Intertropical Convergence Zone
tropical depression
monsoon   tropical storm
storm surge   typhoon

| Level 1 | Level 2 | Level 3 |

Tropical Rain

Rainy areas in the tropics are the result of two processes. One is the Intertropical Convergence Zone (ITCZ), an area where winds from different directions merge (see page 16). The air is forced upward, forming many showers and thunderstorms. The ITCZ is near the equator, but it spreads north in the summer and south in the winter in the Northern Hemisphere. It especially waters central Africa and the rain forests of Brazil.

The second rain process is the monsoon, in which certain areas of the tropics receive drenching rains for six months and are dry for the next six months. The six months of rain are called a monsoon. It is caused by the seasonal changes over the continents. Many tropical areas have monsoon climates, but India is the most well-known. As Asia cools in winter, cool, dry air flows down the Himalaya Mountains, over India, and out into the Indian Ocean. The air is dry because it comes from the continent and sinks down the mountains. During the summer, Asia becomes very warm, and the air flow reverses. This causes air from the Indian Ocean to move northward into India and up the Himalaya Mountains. Since this air comes from the warm Indian Ocean, it is very moist. Moving over land, the air is forced to rise, forming torrential rain. This rain lasts while Asia is warm. Monsoons usually come with lots of flooding, but since they occur every year, the people are normally prepared. The monsoon has caused most of the rainfall records on earth.

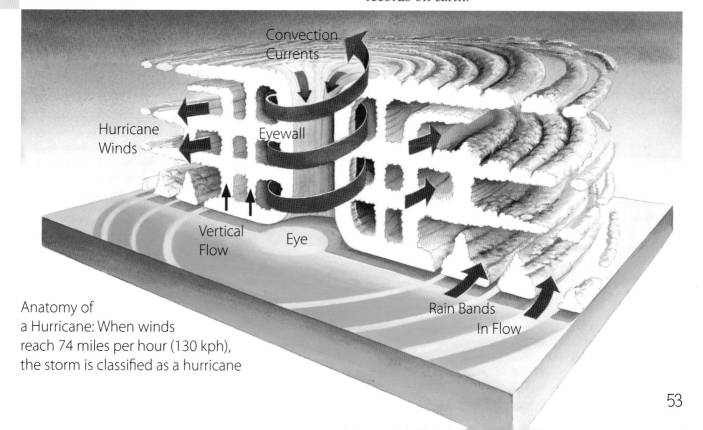

Convection Currents

Hurricane Winds

Eyewall

Vertical Flow

Eye

Rain Bands In Flow

Anatomy of a Hurricane: When winds reach 74 miles per hour (130 kph), the storm is classified as a hurricane

Tropical Storms

Three types of storms in the tropics.		wind speed
tropical depression	rainstorm	38 mph or less (60 kph)
tropical storm	heavy rain	39 and 74 mph (60 to 120 kph)
hurricane	very heavy rain	75 mph or greater (120 kph)

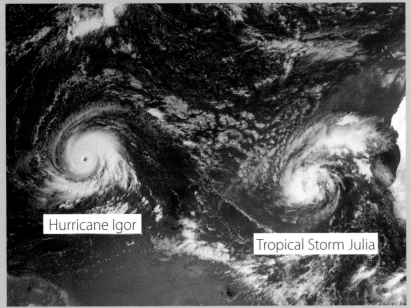

Hurricane Igor

Tropical Storm Julia

Since hurricanes are so destructive, weathermen from all over the world have studied them. They hope their work will help save lives by giving early warnings. Some people who study hurricanes are called hurricane hunters — pilots who fly into the storm and track it. As they fly into a hurricane, they drop special parachute-borne weather sensors into the storm. These sensors measure the storm characteristics beneath the plane. Messages from the sensors are sent back to the plane. This is very important information because it provides a detailed look at the storm's structure. It takes observations to make predictions on future hurricane movement and development.

Researchers have learned that most hurricanes form after the ocean water warms up past 80°F (27°C). That's why hurricanes north of the equator occur between June and November and vice versa for the Southern Hemisphere. Warm water evaporates more quickly than cold water, so the air above has high amounts of vapor. As you recall, water vapor that condenses to form cloud droplets gives off latent heat into the air. This heat is added to the tropical air that is already warm. This causes a large pulse of heat to rise high into the atmosphere. If the winds at the surface and high in the atmosphere travel in the same direction, it causes the warm air to concentrate in one spot. The combination of heat and moisture forms bands of spiraling thunderstorms. As they spin, they blow inward toward the center. The rain is very heavy in these bands. Between bands, it is either raining lightly or not at all. The most violent band with the heaviest rain is the eyewall, which surrounds the eye or center of the hurricane. The eye is normally about 15 miles (24 km) in diameter. The eye is caused by a strong downdraft that dissipates the clouds. All the updrafts in the hurricane caused by the thunderstorms spread out when they hit the stratosphere to form a nearly continuous cloud shield above the storm.

By this time the barometric pressure in the middle of the mass has dropped, causing the wind to increase. Wind from the thunderstorms whips the ocean water into a spray. This, in turn, increases evaporation from the ocean, adding more water vapor into the air, which adds more heat as it condenses. This results in the air pressure dropping even more, making the winds blow even harder. Within a few days the heat, moisture, pressure, and wind whip each other into a full-blown hurricane.

When a hurricane moves inland or over colder water, it quickly weakens and falls apart. It loses contact with what started and fed the whole process — warm ocean water. Torrential rains, however, may continue even after the wind slows. Tornadoes sometimes occur. The reason some hurricanes survive as far north as New England is because a warm ocean current, called the Gulf Stream, continues to provide energy to the storm.

United States Hurricanes

Generally, six hurricanes a year form in the North Atlantic tropical zone. These storms are pushed by upper winds at about 15 to 20 mph (24–32 kph) toward the west. Only about two of these storms travel as far north as the east coast of the United States. The other four hurricanes are pushed into the Caribbean Sea or into the Gulf of Mexico. Once in a great while, a storm curves as far north as New England. Fortunately, by the time it gets that far it has lost some of its energy.

Hurricanes that form in the Pacific Ocean off Central America normally move westward. Most of them run out of energy before they reach halfway across the Pacific Ocean. Once in a great while, upper winds blow a hurricane north to northwest to southern California. Even though they aren't as strong when they travel north, they still cause heavy rain and flooding. For example, by the time Hurricane Norman reached southern California in 1978, it was downgraded to a tropical depression. Even so, it caused about $500 million in damage.

Since the 1920s, the average number of deaths in the United States from hurricanes has decreased.

The saving of lives was due not only to better hurricane forecasts, but also because of hurricane preparedness efforts. People at all levels of emergency services spend years educating people, planning evacuation routes, and building special shelters. Before Hurricane Andrew struck, 2 million people were evacuated to safety in Florida and Louisiana.

Although many lives are being saved, property damage has increased greatly since the 1920s. Hurricane Andrew alone caused $25 billion in damage. This is partly due to more people living in hurricane-prone areas. One problem is that many people have built homes in very vulnerable locations. Millions live next to the beach. Some have built on low barrier islands offshore. Fortunately, hurricanes are rather rare; the very strong ones, like Andrew, even more rare. The worst part of the hurricane, the eye, impacts only a small part of the coast. As more people build in vulnerable areas, a greater chance exists that more people will be killed in hurricanes.

Flood waters during Hurricane Katrina

Hurricane Gonzalo Viewed From
the International Space Station
October 16, 2014.
Image Credit: Alexander Gerst/ESA/NASA

Hurricane Names

Hurricanes occur in other parts of the tropics. However, different names are used for the storms by other countries. In Japan and the Philippines, hurricanes are called typhoons. In the Indian Ocean, they called tropical cyclones.

For several hundred years, many hurricanes in the Caribbean were named after a particular saint on whose feast day the hurricane struck. For example, the hurricane that hit Puerto Rico on July 26, 1825, was named "Hurricane Santa Ana."

Before the turn of the 20th century, an Australian weatherman named tropical storms after women. This idea caught on, and pretty soon most of the world was giving hurricanes women's names. This practice came to an end in the United States in 1979. Maybe the women decided that men should share the honor of having destructive storms named after them. Since then, hurricanes have been named alphabetically about five years in advance. Each ocean has its own set of names to choose from. The names switch back and forth from women to men. The naming does not begin until the storm has reached the tropical storm stage.

Hurricane Forecasting

For most of U.S. history, hurricanes came without warning. Many ships at sea were surprised by hurricanes and sank. Much treasure from old ships still lies on the ocean bottom, thanks to hurricanes. We can thank God that those days are over. The Galveston and other hurricane disasters prompted the U.S. government to establish a hurricane warning branch. Over the years, hurricane forecasting has greatly improved. In 1943, a hurricane forecast center was established in Miami, Florida. The National Weather Service's National Hurricane Center has since been moved to Coral Gables, Florida. There, the latest computer technology and most sophisticated atmospheric weather programs are run on high-speed computers. Their job is to predict a hurricane's size, intensity, movement, and storm surge. The Center issues a hurricane watch if it is believed the hurricane will hit a certain area within 24 to 36 hours. A hurricane warning is issued if the storm is forecast to hit within 24 hours or less. Hurricanes are classified according to intensity, with level 1 as the weakest and level 5 as the strongest.

Satellites, 22,000 miles out in space, can see hurricanes form and watch their movement. Hurricanes are easy to recognize. They look like giant cloud doughnuts or pinwheels. They can now be detected long before they reach the U.S. coastline. Satellite information also is used as input into the computer models, which forecasts its track. When a hurricane draws near, many coastal Doppler weather radars track the storm's details.

Massive Destruction by Hurricanes

Hurricanes are the most destructive storms on earth. A hurricane is over 500 miles wide and sets in motion about a million cubic miles of atmosphere. They generate an enormous amount of energy. If we could change the energy of just one hurricane into electricity, the United States would have enough electric power to last three years!

In a hurricane, the wind can gust over 200 mph (320 kph). However, it isn't the wind that causes the most deaths in a hurricane. Rather, it's the rising ocean water rushing onto the land that accounts for 90 percent of the deaths. Extremely low air barometric pressure inside some hurricanes causes the sea to rise one to three feet (up to a meter) above normal. Normal sea level pressure is around 30.00 in. (76 cm) of mercury. The lowest reading on many barometers is 28.00 in. (71 cm). In many hurricanes, the barometer needle moves way off the end of the scale. The lowest sea level pressure ever recorded on earth was 25.69 in. (65 cm) in Typhoon Tip on October 12, 1979. The low pressure acts like a big vacuum cleaner sucking up the ocean water. As the water rises, strong winds whip it into huge waves, sometimes 50 to 60 feet high (15 to 18 m). The winds are so strong they cause the water to heap up against the shore and pour over the land. This is called a storm surge. These surges can be 15 to 25 feet (5 to 8 m) higher than the normal ocean level. As the water spreads inland, the few people who refuse to leave their homes for higher ground often drown.

Storm surges severely erode beaches, destroy coastal highways, and damage marinas where ships and pleasure boats are tied up. Salt water, when it moves inland, can contaminate lakes and wells. The salt water is poison for animals and people. After Hurricane Andrew struck, snakes crazy from salt poisoning slithered frantically out of Louisiana's flooded bayous and onto roads.

Notable Hurricanes

Tornadoes and severe thunderstorms usually happen after the hurricane moves onshore. These storms occur mostly around the hurricane's edge.

Tropical Cyclone Sidr

The worst hurricane in the 20th century occurred in the Indian Ocean. On November 12, 1970, a hurricane moved north from the Bay of Bengal into Bangladesh. On that stormy day a 25-foot (8 m) wall of water (the storm surge) struck its shore. Since Bangladesh is very flat, the water rushed over the land, burying everything in its way. The country was devastated, as 300,000 to 500,000 people died. Most of the remaining population was left homeless. Since the country is so poor, there was no communication system in place to warn them. They had no place to go even if they were warned, since there are no mountains in southern Bangladesh. After the storm, many countries came to their aid. Bangladesh is especially vulnerable to disastrous hurricanes because it is in the tropics, near an ocean, and on flat land. Another less-damaging hurricane struck the country in 1991, killing around 138,000 people.

1900 Galveston Texas Hurricane

In 1900, Galveston, Texas, experienced the deadliest natural disaster in U.S. history. Galveston is an important U.S. port, located on a long, thin island of sand two miles off the Texas coast. Late that summer a hurricane hit Galveston without warning. A huge wall of water flooded the city within minutes. Most of the city was destroyed; 7,200 people died. Shortly after the storm the people decided to fight back. They worked night and day to raise the level of the land. They hauled tons of dirt onto their island. They then built cement bulwarks on the Gulf side of the island. So far, these efforts have protected the city from the ocean surges that come with hurricanes.

Hurricane Iniki

The year 1992 was a bad one for hurricanes in the United States. Hurricane Iniki developed in the Pacific Ocean off the Central American coast. It battered Hawaii, causing $2 billion in damage. The year 2005 was a record-breaking one for hurricanes. Twenty-eight tropical and subtropical storms, 15 became hurricanes; five Category 4 and four Category 5.

58

Hurricane Andrew

Hurricane Andrew struck southern Florida on August 24, 1992. Winds on the ground were reported at 145 mph (232 kph) and gusting to 175 mph (280 kph). It moved west before turning north into Louisiana. Andrew wrecked 60,000 homes and left 200,000 people homeless. The damage was estimated at $25 billion. But thanks to an early warning, only 15 people died in Florida and 8 in Louisiana as a direct result of the storm. Hurricane Andrew caused a total of 61 tornadoes and 177 severe storms. Amazingly enough, only 2 people were killed and a few injured by these associated tornadoes and thunderstorms.

Hurricane Katrina

Hurricane Katrina, which hit the Gulf Coast in late August of 2005, was the costliest natural disaster in the United States at $108 billion, and one of the five deadliest hurricanes. 1,833 fatalities occurred from the hurricane and the flooding afterward by the catastrophic breaking of the Mississippi River dikes at New Orleans, LA.

Hurricane Sandy

Hurricane Sandy was the most unusual hurricane to hit the United States. It occurred in the eastern United States in late October of 2012. Although the hurricane was only of moderate intensity, it combined with a strong low-pressure system and mushroomed into "Superstorm Sandy." Hurricane Sandy affected 24 states from Florida to Maine and west into Wisconsin. Flooding by the storm surge was substantial, including the streets, tunnels, and subway lines in and around the New York City. Total damage in the United States was $65 billion, the second-costliest natural disaster.

Hurricane SAFETY TIPS

If a hurricane watch is issued:
- Turn the refrigerator to the coldest setting to preserve food longer.
- Keep your car fueled.
- Have plenty of emergency supplies stored, such as canned food, batteries, propane for camp stoves, extra money, etc.
- Fill water bottles and the bathtub with water.

- Review family evacuation plans.
- Bring pets indoors.
- Bring outdoor objects inside the house or garage.
- Make sure medical supplies are available.

If a hurricane warning is issued:
- Board up windows and garage.
- Unplug appliances
- Be prepared to evacuate.

07 | Winter Storms

Snow is a wonderful creation by God; it is not only beautiful but also useful. It gently floats from the sky, each delicate flake having its own unique crystalline shape. The snow creates a fluffy, protective blanket for plants, seeds, and tiny animals, shielding them from the harsh winter. It is fun to play in and sled down hills.

High in the mountains, storm after storm piles the snow deeper and deeper. This snowpack becomes nature's water preserve. In the spring it will gradually melt and replenish the rivers, streams, reservoirs, and groundwater.

Words to Know

ice storm	ice jam
sleet	Northeaster
wind chill factor	frostbite
blizzard	hypothermia
avalanche	inversion

Level 1	Level 2	Level 3

Seasonal Changes

Seasons determine the type of weather during the year. Most areas have four seasons. In the previous chapters, we have discussed warm weather storms, but winter storms occur during the cold season and are very different.

The seasons are caused by the earth's tilt on its axis as it orbits around the sun. The earth's axis is an imaginary line that goes from the North Pole to the South Pole. The earth rotates once every 24 hours on this axis, which tilts at a 23.5 degree angle. The tilt causes daylight hours to grow shorter as winter approaches.

In the winter, less sunshine during short days and long nights cause, cooler temperatures, especially at mid and high latitudes. The shortest day of the year in the Northern Hemisphere is at the end of December. In the far north, near the North Pole, there is no sunshine during much of the winter, so the polar areas become very cold.

As the earth continues its yearly course around the sun, winter changes to summer, and the days soon become longer. Long days give the sun more time to warm the ground and atmosphere. The long days of sunshine give us summer warmth. The tropics either have no seasons or very small changes in temperature, so they stay warm most of the time. However, a seasonal change in precipitation occurs in many areas. The heavy precipitation in the tropics can be caused either by the Intertropical Convergence Zone (ITCZ) or the monsoon.

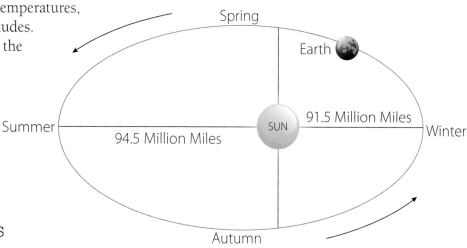

Different Climates

Thunderstorms occur less during autumn. In the Northern Hemisphere, the hurricane season ends around December 1. As temperatures drop, rain and snowstorms are more frequent, usually lasting a day or two and bringing large amounts of moisture. Geography decides which it will be. Snow usually falls in the northern section of North America, Europe, and Asia. Rain generally falls farther south, closer to the equator. The west coasts of the United States, Canada, and Europe rarely experience snow. Relatively warm winds from the ocean blow onto the land, keeping it too warm for snow. Although Ireland is far north, the warm Gulf Stream current causes mild winters with little snow.

The climate on North America's east coast differs from the west coast. This is because the prevailing west wind on the east coast blows from off the snowy continent bringing, the cold, wintry air with it. The warm Atlantic Ocean doesn't modify this situation much because the winds usually blow from the wrong direction.

Why Is Snow White?

Have you ever wondered why God made snow white? He did it for a special reason. When sunlight glistens on the snow, most of its rays are reflected into space. This reflection is called the albedo of the snow and is "1" for perfectly reflecting snow and "0" for total absorption of sunlight. The high albedo allows the snow to melt slowly. The melt water then percolates deep into the soil. This gradual melting makes flooding minimal.

The Donner Party

Many famous winter storms are part of North America's history. In 1846 the Donner Party journeyed by covered wagon from Illinois, headed for Sutter's Fort near Sacramento, California. As a result of bad decisions and slow going, they tried to cross the high Sierra Nevada Mountains in late October. Usually, California is still fairly warm at that time of year. As the party surveyed the Sierra Nevada Mountains, they did not see any snow. However, shortly after they left, huge snowstorms hit the mountains. They were forced to camp near Truckee, California. The snow was so deep their wagon wheels became stuck. It was very cold. They tried to wait the storm out, but when one storm ended, another began. Their supplies dwindled. Some of the party decided to hike out and find help rather than starve. Most of them died in the attempt. Many of those who stayed behind lived. Of the 87 people who started in Illinois, only 47 survived.

The Dangers of Storms

The universe enjoys harmony and beauty, but once in a while a wild storm here or there shows that all is not perfect. Our world has been contaminated with sin; because of that not everything works as God originally planned. Just as some summer storms become dangerous, so also do some winter storms. It is wise to know how to protect ourselves from these events.

Most winter rainstorms in the southern United States are a blessing. The rain soaks deep into the ground to be used the next spring for growing crops. Winter rains add water to streams, rivers, springs, and wells. However, in California heavy rain storms cause problems. For example, because southern California is so far south, its winter air is warm. Warmer air can hold more water vapor. Southern California is also next to the ocean, close to

the vapor source. So its winter rains are especially heavy. Rain pours even harder on the mountains and hills around Los Angeles. After the normally dry land becomes soaked, little streams of water course their way down the hillsides and erode the soil on the way. In the worst conditions, these streams cause mudslides to sweep down the hills. The problem becomes especially serious after a forest or brush fire destroys the soil-stabilizing vegetation. Many people have built houses on these hillsides. Sometimes after heavy rains, the soil and their homes slide down the hill.

Snowstorms are exciting and beautiful, but if people do not know their dangers they can be injured or die. When a winter storm begins, it is wiser to watch it from your window than to be outside. Snow in a storm can fall very fast and is often whipped into large drifts.

A snowstorm is called a blizzard when the winds are over 35 mph (56 kph), and you can't see ahead because of blowing and falling snow.

Winter storms and blizzards can deposit several feet of snow that blows into huge drifts. Sometimes the drifts are over ten feet tall. They can even cover a house. Winter storms can completely paralyze a city; stranding people at airports, stopping the flow of supplies, and disrupting emergency services. They can cause power poles and trees to topple. Extremely heavy snow can even cave in a roof. People who live in rural areas, especially, may be isolated for days. Cows and sheep can become stranded and die of the cold. In the mountains, heavy snow sometimes leads to avalanches. The arctic cold that comes behind a winter storm can cause ice jams on rivers and streams.

The Storm of the Century

On March 12–15, 1993, a winter storm, now called the "Storm of the Century," struck eastern North America. A huge blizzard developed in the northern Gulf of Mexico then curved northeast up the east coast. Fortunately for the East, this kind of storm hits only once in a hundred years. The last storm of this size hit the northeastern United States in 1888. The 1993 storm was a powerful Northeaster — a storm that moves northeast along the east coast. The winds ahead of the storm are from the east to northeast and pick up large amounts of water vapor from the warm Gulf Stream Current. All this water vapor ends up as heavy rain close to the ocean and deep snow inland.

The Storm of the Century affected the entire east coast. It caused 15 tornadoes and severe thunderstorms in Florida which killed 44 people. The wind and low pressure caused a 12-foot-high storm surge to hit the east coast. Six inches (15 cm) of snow fell on the Florida panhandle in March, which is unusual.

As the storm ripped northeast up the east coast, heavy wet snow was driven by strong hurricane-force winds. The winds piled the snow into huge drifts. When the snow stopped, it totaled 56 inches (142 cm) deep in Mount LeConte, TN. It was 50 inches (127 cm) on Mount Mitchell, NC; 44 inches (112 cm) in Snowshoe, WV; 43 inches (109 cm) at Syracuse, NY; 36 inches (91 cm) at Latrobe, NH; 29 inches (74 cm) in Page County, VA; 24 inches (61 cm) in Mountain City, GA; 19 inches (48 cm) at Portland, ME; and 17 inches (43 cm) near Birmingham, AL.

The highest winds gusted to 131 mph (210 kph) at Grand Etang, Nova Scotia. In many other areas from Florida to southeast Canada the winds gusted over 70 mph (112 kph). Hundreds of roofs collapsed, thousands of people were stranded, and millions were without electricity. For the first time in U.S. history, every major airport on the east coast was closed at one time or another because of the storm. Interstate highways from Atlanta northward were closed, two ships sank, and the pounding surf destroyed houses along the coast. At least 270 people were killed, and 48 were missing at sea — three times the combined death toll from Hurricanes Andrew and Hugo. Property damage was estimated at $5 billion. It was the country's costliest winter storm ever.

March 12-14, 1993
Snowfall (inches)
1 - 4 4 - 10 10 - 20 20 - 30 30+
NESIS = 13.20
Category 5

How Temperature Affects Winter Precipitation

SNOW
28°
29°
30°
31°
31°
30°
30°

Cloud temperature is cold enough for snow to form: air above ground does not melt it.

SLEET
34°
33°
32°
31°
30°
30°
30°

Rain freezes to ice pellets and can pile up like snow: This can be a serious road hazard.

FREEZING RAIN
36°
35°
34°
33°
32°
31°
30°

Rain falls onto a below-freezing surface and forms a glaze of ice. Very hazardous!

Winter storms can be dangerous for a number of reasons. Frostbite and hypothermia can occur. When a severe wind chill factor is in operation, a person's exposed skin can freeze. When people have frostbite, their skin becomes pale and numb. The most susceptible parts of the body are fingers, toes, ear lobes, and the tip of the nose. Hypothermia happens when a person is out in the cold so long that the body temperature drops below normal. He or she starts shivering and is unable to stop. The person then becomes confused and forgets where he or she is. Speech becomes slurred, and the words don't make sense. Soon he or she becomes very tired and wants to sleep, anywhere. If someone gets hypothermia, wrap the victim in blankets and take him or her to the hospital emergency ward. If it's impossible to get to a hospital quickly, do all you can to gradually warm the individual.

Winter storms are considered deceptive killers because most deaths are indirectly related to the storm. For example, 70 percent of all winter deaths are the result of accidents involving people driving on icy and dangerous roads. Another 25 percent of storm-related deaths happen to people caught outside in storms with no shelter available. The core body temperature falls, and the victim dies of hypothermia. Most

of that 25 percent who die are men over 40 years old. Some people die of heart attacks while shoveling snow.

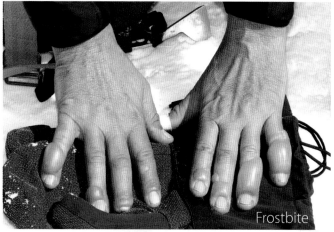

Frostbite

65

Ice Storms

Also dangerous are ice storms, caused by rain falling into the lower atmosphere that is below freezing. This temperature condition near the ground is called an inversion. The air above is warmer than the air close to the ground. When raindrops fall into the lower layer of below-freezing air, they become supercooled but not frozen. Supercooled drops freeze when they are jostled or hit an object. Sometimes the raindrops freeze before they hit the ground. These are called ice pellets or sleet. Ice pellets are not nearly as dangerous as freezing rain.

When drops of liquid rain freeze on objects, a shimmering layer of ice coats everything. Cities are transformed into crystal palaces. Icicles drip from trees and telephone wires. Ice covers roads and cars. The ice glimmers and sparkles in the sun. It is beautiful but nearly impossible to drive or walk on. Walking on sidewalks of ice becomes a slippery adventure. Once in a while, telephone or electrical wires snap from the weight of the ice. After a freezing rainstorm, avoid broken electrical lines.

Cause of Winter Storms

Winter storms are caused by a strong temperature difference between the tropics and the mid and high latitudes. The mid-latitudes range from approximately 35° to 60° latitude. In the Northern Hemisphere the high latitudes extend from 60° latitude to the North Pole. As winter approaches, the earth cools in the mid and high latitudes. The cooling creates a large temperature difference between the tropics and the poles. For instance, a change in temperature from Texas to northern Saskatchewan, Canada, can be 100°F (56°C). When strong temperature differences are concentrated in a small area, they create a front. If the front is not moving, it is a stationary front. The jet stream is caused by the difference in temperature. A winter storm needs a small "instability" to get started, and then it can amplify. As the storm becomes stronger, the jet stream guides the storm, usually from the west to east. When the warm air moves northward ahead of the storm it is a warm front, when cold air moves southward behind the storm it is a cold front.

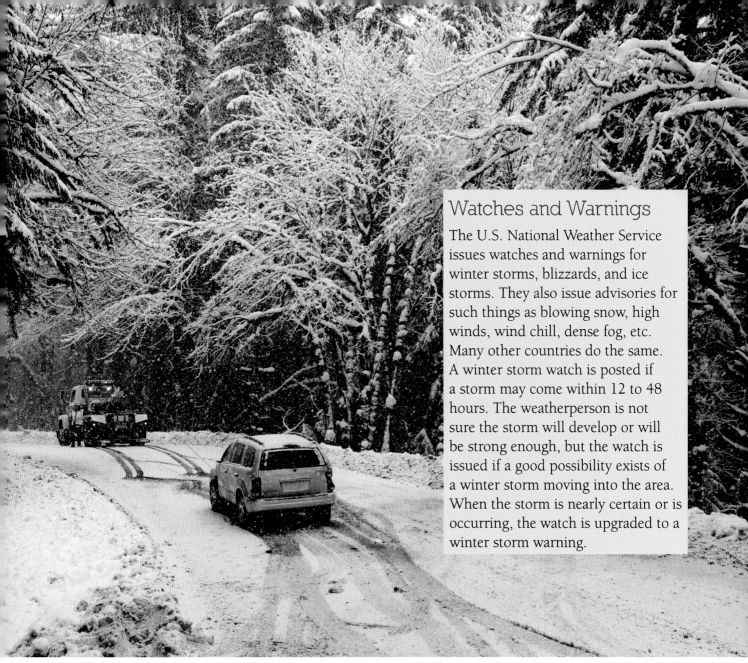

Watches and Warnings

The U.S. National Weather Service issues watches and warnings for winter storms, blizzards, and ice storms. They also issue advisories for such things as blowing snow, high winds, wind chill, dense fog, etc. Many other countries do the same. A winter storm watch is posted if a storm may come within 12 to 48 hours. The weatherperson is not sure the storm will develop or will be strong enough, but the watch is issued if a good possibility exists of a winter storm moving into the area. When the storm is nearly certain or is occurring, the watch is upgraded to a winter storm warning.

Winter Storm SAFETY TIPS

- Make sure you have enough stored food, and batteries for a radio and flashlight in either your house or car.

- Avoid unnecessary travel.

- If you must go outside, dress with several layers of warm clothes. Do not overexert yourself, such as shoveling snow, pushing a car, or walking in deep snow. Sweating could lead to a chill and hypothermia. Find shelter. Cover all of the exposed parts of your body, and try to keep dry. Wait calmly for the storm to end; they usually don't last too long without a break.

- If you must drive, carry sleeping bags for every person and keep your gas tank full. Let someone know your destination.

- If you get stuck, stay in your vehicle. Remain visible to rescuers by keeping an overhead light on, and attach a bright-colored cloth to your antenna. As you sit in the car, move around to keep warm. You can run the engine and heater for a brief period, but check to be sure the exhaust pipe is not plugged. Also, keep one window slightly cracked to prevent carbon monoxide poisoning.

When people think of Hawaii, they think of beautiful white, sandy beaches and basking in the warm sunshine. But one point in the Hawaiian Islands has one of the highest yearly rainfalls in the world. Mount Waialeale, on the north-western island of Kauai, receives an average of 460 inches (1,168 cm) of rain per year. That's almost 40 feet (12 m) of rain annually!

Hawaii has unique mountainous geography and plentiful sunshine. The atmosphere around the islands carries a large amount of water vapor. Northeast trade winds gently blow across the tropical ocean, picking up huge amounts of water vapor. As the winds move up the mountains on Kauai, the wet air cools and condenses into clouds. As the day becomes warmer, the clouds quickly develop into thunderstorms. Slow upper winds give them plenty of time to release their moisture generously. That's why Mt. Waialeale experiences so much rain.

Mount Waialeale (Wai'ale'ale), Kauai.

Words to Know

ball lightning	trade winds
chinook winds	foehn winds
Santa Ana winds	rain forest
St. Elmo's fire	lake-effect snow

Level 1	Level 2	Level 3

From Rain Forest to Desert

In Washington state, you can start from a rain forest, travel east over the Cascade Mountains, and enter into a desert — all within several hours. The western slopes of the Olympic Mountains receive so much rain and snow the area is considered to be a rain forest. They collect their abundant rain in the same way as Mt. Waialeale in Hawaii. The rain falls as moisture-laden air climbs the mountains. In Washington State, however, the moisture is cool and comes from the northern Pacific Ocean. Many of the mountains collect over 100 inches (254 cm) of water a year. In fact, the greatest snowfall in any one year in the world is 102 feet (3,150 cm) at Paradise Ranger Station, located at about 5,000 feet (1,525 m) elevation on Mount Rainier in the Cascade Mountains.

As you travel over the Cascade Mountains and down the east side, the climate becomes drier. By the time you reach Yakima or Pasco, Washington, it's practically a desert. Yakima receives only 8 inches (21 cm) of rainfall a year. As the west winds continue east and blow down the Cascade Mountains, the air becomes warmer and drier. Just as rising air cools and becomes more moist, the opposite happens when the air sinks to lower altitudes. Washington State's climate dramatically illustrates the difference a mountain range makes on the weather and climate. The windward side (toward the wind) is a rain forest; the leeward side (away from the wind) is nearly a desert.

Foehn Winds

A foehn (pronounced fone) wind is relatively warm and dry, descending down a mountain slope. They occur in almost all mountain regions of the mid and high latitudes, most frequently during the colder time of year. Foehn winds are common east of the high Andes Mountains. They are well-known in Japan, New Zealand, and eastern and central Asia. Foehn winds also blow from the Greenland Ice Sheet down to the coast. Even Antarctica experiences foehn winds near some mountains. However, these winds are cold.

The word "foehn" originated from the European Alps. Due to storms moving across northern Europe, south and west winds blow down the north and east slopes of the Alps. Even though the winds generally blow strong, the weather is quite mild. Foehn winds are especially prevalent where north-south valleys open onto the plains or in large east-west valleys. It was at Innsbruck, Austria, where foehn winds were actively studied. Besides warmer, drier air, foehn winds typically come with extraordinarily good visibility. The mountains can appear unusually close. Near the mountains, a wall of cumulus-like clouds are observed. These clouds are called the foehn wall. Out from the mountains, lens-shaped clouds at medium levels in the atmosphere are seen. These are called altocumulus lenticularis.

In the United States, especially along the east slopes of the Rocky Mountains from Alberta, Canada, to New Mexico, foehn winds are called chinooks (pronounced shinooks). Chinook is a Native American word meaning "snow eater." These mild, gusty west winds can melt a lot of snow within a few days or less. For long stretches of winter, chinook winds keep the eastern slopes of the Rocky Mountains and the high plains snow-free. Tens of thousands of elk and deer move from their mountain home to spend the winter and find dry grass in these areas.

However, chinook winds occasionally become very strong and dangerous. They can fan grass fires out of control, even in the winter. East Glacier, Montana, and Boulder, Colorado, are well-known for their damaging chinook winds, which have peaked up to 125 mph (200 kph). Trucks and campers are blown off the road every year, and even trains have been derailed around East Glacier and Livingston, Montana. At East Glacier, homes are tied down by hurricane straps. In strong winds, hanging houseplants sway indoors. A cooperative weather observer from East Glacier used to know when the wind exceeded 90 mph (144 kph), because at that speed an old defective toilet would flush.

Diagram of a foehn wind warming the leeward, or sheltered from the wind, side of a mountain range. These winds occur due to the moist air cooling on the windward side at a slower rate than the dry air is heated on the leeward side. This is because water condenses as air rises, releasing latent heat that slows the rate of cooling. The wind heats up so much as it decends on the leeward side, it can raise the surrounding temperature by up to 54 degrees Fahrenheit (30 degrees Celsius) in just a few hours.

Foehn clouds in the distance

The National Weather Service issues a high wind warning for potentially damaging chinook winds.

When cold arctic air from Canada meets the chinook winds, it causes some enormous temperature changes. Browning, Montana, dropped 100°F (56°C) in 24 hours in January 1916. The temperature fell from 44°F (7°C) to -56°F (-49°C). In just 27 minutes, Spearfish, South Dakota, fell 58°F (32°C), from 54°F (12°C) to -4°F (-20°C). It can warm up just as fast when a chinook blows into the area of Arctic air. On January 11, 1981, in Great Falls, Montana, the temperature rose from -32°F (-36°C) to 15°F (-9°C) in just 7 minutes!

This rapid seesaw in temperature causes unusual moisture effects. When arctic air retreats back up into Canada, the sparse water vapor from the chinook wind condenses as frost on the cold pavement. This is dangerous for drivers because, although the road looks dry, it's very slippery. Even car windows will quickly frost when coming from

the cold arctic air into the warm chinook. The cold windshield's contact with the warm chinook air causes rapid condensation of water vapor on the windshield. Suddenly, all the windows turn white. This is dangerous because the driver can't see the road.

Another famous foehn wind is called the Santa Ana wind in California. It blows westward from the mountains of southern California to the coast when a high-pressure area settles over Nevada, Utah, and Idaho. As the air descends down the mountains, temperatures can rise to 100°F (38°C) in winter by the time the wind reaches the coast. In some canyons the wind can blow over 100 mph (160 kph). This is because of the funnel effect caused by wind flowing through a narrow opening in a mountain range. Sometimes these winds pick up massive amounts of dust. The Santa Ana winds are so dry that fires fan out of control. They can occur at any time of the year.

71

Ball Lightning

A very mysterious sight usually associated with thunderstorms is ball lightning — a glowing ball of light. Those who have seen it say it's generally the size and shape of a grapefruit or basketball; it has even been reported to be as large as a car. The glowing ball is either red, orange, or yellow. A few people have seen it falling from the clouds. On occasion, ball lightning hovers or glides just above the ground for a few seconds, or it can roll on the surface of an object. Hissing noises come from the fiery orb. Some have even mistaken it for a UFO.

Ball lightning sometimes explodes loudly, while other times it just quietly fades away. It has been known to pass through an open window, hopping and sizzling across the floor. It can then disappear into electrical outlets, into a television set, or even go up the chimney.

Scientists do not understand ball lightning. Some scientists question the reality of ball lightning since it is so strange. However, it has been widely and long reported in weather journals by trustworthy observers. So, it likely is real.

St. Elmo's Fire

An unusual phenomenon is St. Elmo's Fire. Once in a great while, during a nighttime lightning storm, people look toward the mountains and see eerie glows of light outlining sharp mountain peaks. Pilots occasionally report seeing their wing tips aglow. Unseasoned sailors at sea have been frightened when their ship's mast began to glow.

St. Elmo's Fire is caused by a high charge of electricity in the air. It normally occurs when there are thunderstorms in the area. Electricity in the air causes pointed objects to glow faintly. A person who did not know what it was might think some heavenly being was visiting. St. Elmo's Fire received its name from Mediterranean sailors who regarded it as a visitation by their patron saint, Erasmus, or Elmo. It was thought to be a good omen by the superstitious sailors, because it tends to occur in the last phases of a violent thunderstorm. This is the time when the thunderstorm is decaying, and the ocean is calming down. Often sailors have praised God for the reassurance of St. Elmo's Fire and been awestruck by its beauty.

A lake-effect winter storm hit Buffalo, NY, in November 2014 and brought up to 7 feet of snow on the area.

Great Lakes Weather

In the eastern United States, the sky normally clears after an arctic cold front passes. However, in the Great Lakes area of the United States and Canada, the opposite occurs. Clouds rise as cold and dry arctic air blows over the comparatively warm Great Lakes. The large temperature difference between the arctic air and the lake water causes a high amount of evaporation to occur. The fact that arctic air is very dry enhances its ability to absorb moisture from the lakes. So, when all this water vapor hits the opposite shoreline, it causes heavy snow squalls to form. The faster the wind speed and the longer the wind blows over the water, the heavier the snow. These snowstorms have been known to deposit up to 102 inches (259 cm) of snow in 5 days. The 1976–77 winter was drier than normal in the eastern United States. The colder than normal temperatures, however, caused 467 inches (1,186 cm) of snow to fall at Hooker, New York.

Lake-effect snowstorms can occur at many locations around the Great Lakes. The main area of snow is close to the lake, but snow squalls can drop snow up to 100 miles (160 km) downwind from the water. This explains why Buffalo, New York, receives so much snow. Buffalo is located at the eastern end of Lake Erie. Heavy snow at Buffalo occurs when the wind direction is out of the west, blowing the length of Lake Erie.

St. Joseph lighthouse under ice

Ice fishing in snow storm on frozen Lake Erie

09 | Climate in the Past

Scientists have studied the earth's rocks, ice sheets, and ocean sediments for many years. One reason is to learn about the planet's past climate. Scientists hope that by learning about the climate in the prehistoric past they can predict future climatic changes. Over the years, they have made many perplexing discoveries they have trouble explaining.

Scientists have found abundant evidence from rocks and fossils of warm climates in the past. Some of these warm-climate fossils were found at high latitudes, close to the poles. For instance, dinosaur fossils, along with warm climate trees and mammals, were discovered in Alaska, northern Canada, and Siberia. Dinosaur fossils were also found in Antarctica!

Satellite view of ice forming at Lake Baikal, southern Siberia.

Words to Know

bogs	uniformitarianism
environment	model
permafrost	sedimentary rock
thermometer	water vapor
Ice Age	Little Ice Age
Medieval Warm Period	

Level 1 | Level 2 | Level 3

Strange Past Climate

In northern Canada's Arctic Islands, about 600 miles from the North Pole, scientists have found many fossilized swamp cypress trees. These trees grow today in the warm, humid swamps of Georgia and Florida. They also found fossils of crocodiles, whose descendants mostly live today in tropical locations. The average winter temperature in that cold north region today is -40°F (-40°C).

Hippopotamus fossils have been found in southern England, France, and western Germany. In southern England, reindeer fossils were found close to hippopotamus fossils. Hippopotami normally live in warm regions. Reindeer live in cold regions. These fossils were found in the very top sediment layers associated with the Ice Age.

Crocodiles have been found living in partially dried-up lakes in the western Sahara Desert. Scientists have explored the Sahara Desert and found abundant fossils of hippopotami, elephants, giraffes, crocodiles, and other animals. They also found fossils of fish and clams. They even discovered that humans lived in the Sahara with these animals. There are tens of thousands of rock art pictures painted by men. These pictures show many types of animals, people, and even whole villages that once existed in the Sahara Desert.

Scientists have sent radar beams from satellites through the desert sands of the eastern Sahara. The pictures that came back were startling. They show old river channels, some quite large, in an area that now receives rain once every 50 years! So, the Sahara Desert was once lush and well-watered.

Much evidence exists that at one time huge lakes occupied most arid or semi-arid areas of the world. Like the Sahara Desert, lakes were abundant in the southwestern United States. The Great Salt Lake in Utah was once 800 feet (244 m) deeper and six times its size. You can see distinct shorelines high up on the sides of hills and mountains around the lake. Other lakes existed in Nevada, and at one time Death Valley had a lake. Where did all this water come from?

Scientists have found bones of woolly mammoths in Siberia, as well as in Alaska. They estimate millions of woolly mammoths lived in these regions. Villagers also found bones from woolly rhinoceroses, elk, deer, and many other animals in the same area. A few mammoths were frozen with food inside their stomachs and stuck between their teeth. These animals are associated with the Ice Age, since they are often found in river flood sediments. Also, the bones of woolly mammoths and other animals are commonly found all over the Northern Hemisphere, near the edge of where the ice sheets used to be.

All these woolly mammoth bones in Siberia are very strange. The farther north, the more bones are found. Bones and tusks were even found on the islands and on the shallow ocean bottom of the Arctic Ocean and the Bering Sea. Woolly mammoths required a huge amount of food and probably moderate weather. Why would they have lived in such a place as Siberia and Alaska where the land is frozen most of the year and food in short supply?

During the summer, the frozen ground in that cold region only melts a few feet down. The pooling water creates massive bogs. It would have been nearly impossible for a large animal to walk in the sticky bogs. They would become stuck and die, if they hadn't died of starvation during the winter first. The climate in Siberia and Alaska had to have been vastly different for these animals to have lived there.

The Past is Not Science

It is important to understand that the study of the past is not science. This is because the scientific method requires that past processes, such as past climate, be observed. We cannot repeat or observe the past. For example, we can observe the temperature outside at any moment by looking at the thermometer. That is scientific. If we wanted to know the temperature 5,000 years ago, there is no way we can observe this temperature. Any educated guess we make is not scientific. None of the requirements for the scientific method can be fulfilled when a scientist studies the past, whether he believes in evolution or creation.

The Past Determined by Assumptions

In order to determine the climate of the past, a scientist must make assumptions about the past. From these assumptions, he develops a model. The model is like a model airplane; it is a representation of the real airplane. A model of the past is a representation of what a scientist thinks happened in the past. Then the scientist looks at data he observes in the present world. He tests how well the observed data in the present fits his model. With models, one studies all evidence of the past, including rocks, fossils, the Bible, and other written records.

There are two main models for the past. These models are built on different assumptions. One model is called the Creation-Genesis Flood model. Those who hold to this model believe the Bible gives us an accurate history of the past. They believe that God was the only accurate observer at the time. He is powerful enough to have the past history accurately recorded in His Bible. This model believes that God created everything after its own kind and reproducing after its own kind, and not into some other kind. Those who believe the Creation-Genesis Flood model also believe most of the sedimentary rocks, the layer-caked rocks seen all over the world, were laid down in Noah's worldwide Flood.

The other model is the evolution-uniformitarian model. This model assumes that every organism that has ever lived is a product of millions of years of evolution, and they also believe that the rocks were formed by slow processes of erosion and sedimentation that we observe today. This is where the prefix uniform comes from in uniformitarianism. They believe in uniform or slow processes over millions of years. Uniformitarianism is a good assumption for recent times. However, these scientists extend uniformitarianism to account for all past rocks. This assumption automatically eliminates Noah's Flood.

With two different models and beginning assumptions, a scientist can look at the data we observe at present and draw conclusions about that data. Sometimes scientists, looking at the same data, will draw completely different conclusions. This is because they each believe in a different model.

Island in the city of Irkutsk on the Angara River, Russia

Cathedral Rock in the John Day Fossil Beds National Monument

Applications

The different assumptions and conclusions of the two models are especially important to understand. They can be illustrated by how each looks at sedimentary rocks. Most rocks on the surface of the earth are sedimentary rocks. All of these rocks were once mud, sand, and pebbles that were carried and deposited by water. With time or pressure these sediments hardened and became sandstone, shale, and conglomerate. The sediments form layers, like the layers of a cake.

A geologist can study river erosion processes for many years. He observes the river and studies its banks, its channel, the amount of sediment (dirt the water carries), erosion, and deposition. He concludes that water in the river gradually eroded or wore away the river's banks. He sees that it deposited the sediment a little downriver along the bank, on a flood plain, or carried the sediment into the ocean. This is scientific because he observes these processes happening in the present. However, he then concludes that repeated erosion and deposition of sediments over millions of years explains all the sedimentary rocks in the world, like the great thickness of hardened sediments seen in the Grand Canyon. Of course, if the sediments seen in the Grand Canyon formed by uniform, present process, it would take millions of years to collect. This is one reason scientists who believe the evolution-uniformitarian model believe in millions and billions of years of past earth history.

Scientists who believe the Bible is God's Word know that about 5,000 years ago the earth experienced a gigantic global Flood. The Genesis Flood could easily explain how sedimentary rocks were laid down quickly — not by present processes. It was not a little water over millions of years, but a lot of water over a short period of time. Assuming Noah's Flood took place, evolutionary scientists would be wrong about how the majority of sedimentary rocks were formed. They would also be wrong about how much time it would take to deposit all the sediments, such as the sediments seen in the walls of Grand Canyon.

Evolutionary scientists would also be mistaken about past climates. Fossils of warm-climate animals and plants in polar regions are very difficult to explain by the evolutionary-uniformitarian model. Take, for example, dinosaurs and swamp cypress discovered near the poles. Present processes could not explain such findings. The Creation-Genesis Flood model has several possible explanations for these fossils. There could have been a warm climate in polar regions due to a warmer atmosphere. Or the high latitude animals and plants could also have been swept poleward from tropical locations by powerful currents during the Flood. Both could be true.

Causes of a Warmer Pre-Flood Climate

A pre-Flood warmer climate is a deduction based on the rocks and fossils. Billions of fossils exist in the sedimentary rocks. These fossils commonly have a warm aspect, such as palm and swamp cypress plant fossils. Crocodiles, tortoises, lemurs, and other such animals also reinforce that the pre-Flood environment was warm where these animals lived before the Flood. Such fossils are not only found at low latitudes, where expected, but also at high latitudes. Just the large number of warm-aspect fossils all over the earth tells us the pre-Flood climate was warm.

Another consideration is the amount of coal in the sedimentary rocks. Coal is the compressed accumulation of trees and plants that have been transformed to coal by higher temperatures. The amount of coal can give us an estimate of the amount of trees and plants on the pre-Flood earth. Although estimates vary, it seems like there was about 10 times as much carbon in the form of coal as the current plants and trees on the whole earth. Just think of 10 times the amount of vegetation on the earth before the Flood. All these trees and plants needed to be watered, which implies a very efficient pre-Flood watering system, probably involving underground water under pressure.

Since trees take in carbon dioxide and give off oxygen and water vapor, water vapor in the atmosphere would be much higher than today. Well-watered plants and trees also imply a lot of water on the surface, which would evaporate vapor into the atmosphere. More atmospheric water vapor would cause a large greenhouse effect with the net result of a warmer, more humid pre-Flood climate. The greenhouse effect is the process by which atmospheric gases absorb a little of the sunshine and much of the infrared radiation, heating the air.

Moreover, all this pre-Flood vegetation implies small mountains, compared to today, in order to fit so many plants and trees on the land (some trees undoubtedly also grew in shallow water). Low elevations for the land would also result in warmer surface temperatures.

The Flood Caused the İce Age

We know that the Ice Age followed the Flood. Ice Age debris is found on top of Flood-deposited rocks and shows features that the Flood could not cause. The worldwide Flood set the stage for the Ice Age. Due to a much different geography and the effects of the Flood, the climate would have been very different for a while after the Flood. It would have caused the Ice Age in which 30 percent of the land at mid and high latitude had snow and ice. Today only 10 percent of the land is ice-bound, namely Greenland and Antarctica.

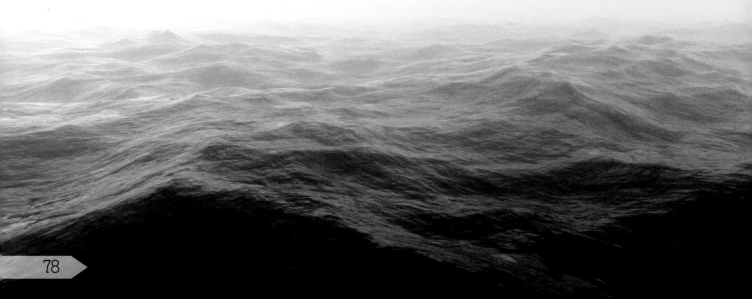

The Cause of the Ice Age

What is required for an ice age to happen? There are two main requirements that must persist for a long time. These are colder summers and much more snowfall. Winters are already cold enough at most locations where the ice sheets existed in the past.

During the Flood, many volcanic eruptions occurred. Volcanoes would have continued erupting after the Flood. Volcanic ash and gases would have reflected much of the warm sunshine back to space, cooling the ground. Summers would have been much colder over the land. The oceans would have been very warm after the Flood. Hot water would have been added to the pre-Flood ocean from the "fountains of the great deep." Volcanoes, lava flows, and earth movements would have added more heat. The ocean water would have been warm all the way to the poles. The Arctic Ocean could have had a temperature of 80°F (27°C) for a while. You could have taken a swim in the Arctic Ocean.

Maximum extent of the Ice Age.

The warmer the water, the more the evaporation. Enormous amounts of water vapor rose from the warm ocean and blew onto the cool continents. Snow fell in the northern latitudes year around. Snow piled up as storm after storm blew onto the continents. Eventually the sheer weight of the snow compacted into ice. Soon, ice sheets developed over northern North America, northern Europe, and northwest Asia. Greenland and Antarctica developed ice sheets that we can still see today.

With time, volcanic eruptions slowed down, and the ocean temperature became cooler. More sunlight reached the ground. Less water evaporated from cooler oceans. So the Ice Age quickly ended. It only lasted about 700 years. There was only one Ice Age because there was only one Flood that changed the climate. There also will never be another ice age. (For more information, see the author's children's book: *Life in the Great Ice Age.*)

Yosemite valley was shaped by an Ice Age glacier.

The Ice Age Explains Many Climate Mysteries

Scientists who believe in the evolution-uniformitarian model have difficulty accounting for the Ice Age. It is extremely difficult for ice sheets to form in the present climate. It would take a summer cooling of around 50° F (28° C) in the northern United States with much more snowfall. However, since cooler air is drier, there is a problem getting the needed snowfall. That is why more than 60 theories have been invented to try to account for the Ice Age. All these theories have serious difficulties.

The Ice Age caused by the Genesis Flood can explain many of the perplexing mysteries of the past. The evolution-uniformitarian model has been unable to explain these mysteries. Consider the hippopotamus fossils found in western Europe. During the beginning of the Ice Age, hippopotami would be able to migrate to southern England because of the proximity to the warm ocean water. The warm Atlantic Ocean would bathe western Europe in warm air with much more rainfall. Eventually, as the climate turned colder, the hippos would die and end up fossilized along with reindeer, musk oxen, and woolly mammoths in Ice Age deposits.

Storm tracks would have been different during the post-Flood Ice Age. Tropical weather patterns would also have been different. The Sahara had a wet climate and bloomed with animals and people after the Flood. Unfortunately, at the end of the Ice Age the weather patterns changed to what they are now. The Sahara gradually became a desert. The animals either migrated or died of starvation or thirst. A few crocodiles were able to survive in partially dried up lakes at high elevations of the western Sahara into the 19th and 20th centuries. These crocodiles show that the change in the Sahara Desert occurred not that long ago.

Both the Genesis Flood and the Ice Age can explain the abundant evidence of lakes and rivers that once existed in areas that are now desert. The initial filling of the lakes is easily explained by the Flood. When the Flood waters receded, basins that had no outlets would remain filled with water. During the Ice Age the much wetter climate would maintain the lakes with streams and rivers for at least several hundred years. After the Ice Age, the lakes would mostly dry up. The evolution-uniformitarian model has serious difficulty filling up these lakes in a cool, dry Ice Age climate. Their model requires at least six times more water flowing into the Great Salt Lake for the water level to rise 800 feet (244 m).

As you may have realized, the creation-Genesis Flood model can explain the woolly mammoths in Siberia by the unique Ice Age climate after the Flood. A warm Arctic and North Pacific Ocean would have kept Siberia, as well as Alaska, comfortable during winter. As a result these areas would have no permafrost and no massive summer bogs. The moisture from the warm oceans would have kept these areas well-watered. Vegetation would be lush, so the animals would have had plenty to eat. But towards the end of the Ice Age, the oceans would cool, and the climate of Siberia would become colder and drier. The Arctic Ocean would have quickly frozen. Cold snowstorms devastated many of the woolly mammoths. The permafrost formed and preserved their remains. The climate of Siberia and Alaska has remained cold to this day. (For more information, see the author's children's book: *Uncovering the Mysterious Woolly Mammoth.*)

Summary

The geological and fossil evidence shows that the climate was much different in the past. By relying on present processes as the key to the past, the evolutionary-uniformitarian model is inadequate to explain these climate mysteries. However, the Creation-Genesis Flood model can easily explain these observations. Solving these many mysteries marvelously points to the fact that there was a mighty global Flood as described in the Bible. Not only that, the Flood resulted in a unique climate and Ice Age right after the Flood.

Lake Baikal
Russia.

Historical Climate Change

Not only was there a great Ice Age, but there also was a Little Ice Age. Before that was the Medieval Warm Period—a period of above average temperatures from around A.D. 800 to 1300, This was the time the Vikings settled southwest Greenland and farmed the land.

However, the warm climate changed to below normal temperatures from about 1300 to 1880. This is called the Little Ice Age, and practically all the glacier in the world advanced. The average snow level in the atmosphere was around 330 feet (100 m) lower than today. The Thames River that runs through London, England, froze up many of those years, which is unheard of today.

The cause of the Little Ice Age can be related to increased volcanism and effects on the sun. Strong volcanoes add sulfur dioxide to the atmosphere which turns to sulfuric acid with the addition of water vapor. It is these small sulfuric acid particles in the stratosphere that reflect some of the sunlight back to space, cooling the surface. A little more volcanism during the Little Ice Age would have caused slightly cooler temperatures.

Effects on the sun can be tracked by the number of sunspots. When there are fewer sunspots than average, slightly less heat comes from the sun. There are also more cosmic rays from outer space that strike the earth affecting the clouds. Since the climate system is so complicated, it is not known exactly how these effects result in slightly cooler temperatures. Regardless, a low number of sunspots can be related to the Little Ice Age. In fact, there was a period from 1645 to 1715, called the Maunder minimum, when there were hardly any sunspots at all at a time there should have been tens of thousands. This period of the Maunder minimum was one of the most severe of the Little Ice Age.

10 | Climate Change

The climate is the average weather at a location. For instance, we know it is cold in the winter in Siberia and hot at the equator. This is the climate, which seems constant. However, the climate can change; it does not stay constant.

We have had both drastic and small climate changes in the past, as shown in chapter 9. We had a warm pre-Flood climate that changed after the Flood. There was a great Ice Age after the Flood. Climate change has been small ever since the melting of the great ice sheets, for instance with the Medieval Warm Period and the Little Ice Age.

Words to Know

El Niño	ultraviolet light
fossil fuels	climate
ozone	La Niña
plankton	heat-island effect
pollution	
greenhouse effect warming	

Level 1	Level 2	Level 3

Small Climate Changes Today

The climate system of the earth is very complicated. Variables within this system can cause small climate changes. We know that large volcanic eruptions can cause globally cooler temperatures, generally cooling by about 1°F (which equates to 0.6°C) for several years. Although scientists are uncertain about it, they also know that features on the sun, as measured by the number of sunspots, can affect climate. When the number of sunspots is high, it is a little warmer. When the sunspot number is low, it is a bit cooler. Another climate change is El Niño.

El Niño

A cold ocean current, called the Peru current, flows northward along the South American coast of Peru and Ecuador. This water is cold because part of it comes from the deep ocean up to the surface. Deep ocean water contains essential minerals for plankton (small plant and animal organisms). The plankton multiply and become food for fish, which local fishermen catch. This current is caused mostly by winds in the tropical atmosphere. Each year the current changes direction and becomes warmer for a while. The warming normally occurs around Christmas, and that is why the current is called El Niño, which is Spanish for "the boy" or "Christ child." Early the next year the current usually changes direction and becomes cold again.

This sequence normally occurs every year. The people of Peru and Ecuador expect it. Usually, the change does not affect the weather very much. However, every two to seven years the warmer current becomes much warmer than normal. The warm water conditions last from 18 to 24 months. The warmer water comes from the tropical ocean around Indonesia and the Philippine Islands and travels eastward across the Pacific Ocean. The warm water is poor in nutrients, so there are few plankton and, therefore, few fish. The fisherman's life becomes very difficult. The strongest recorded El Niño was in 1982 and 1983. Ocean temperatures rose from 7 to 12°F (or 4 to 7°C) above normal off Peru. When the ocean and atmosphere return to a more normal pattern, El Niño changes to La Niña, the Spanish term for "the girl."

El Niño not only affects fishing off the Peruvian coast, but it also changes the weather in Peru and Ecuador. Usually their climate is similar to that of a desert. However, El Niño brings heavy rains and flooding. These changes occur because rainfall is closely tied to the ocean temperature. The warmer water of El Niño evaporates more water into the atmosphere. This water vapor is carried over land and develops into thunderstorms. The 1982–83 El Niño caused catastrophic flooding and mudslides.

Fishing off the coast of Peru

El Niño Climate Changes

It is well established that El Niño causes climate changes in the Pacific Ocean all around the equator. El Niño likely causes dry weather or drought in India, southeast Africa, and northern South America. Scientists have also thought it may be responsible for climate changes in other parts of the world, as far away as northwest North America. These climate changes last for a year or two. Scientists also believe that El Niño causes the southern United States to be wetter than normal in winter.

North America's connection with El Niño is not as strong as that of Peru and Ecuador because it is farther from the tropical Pacific Ocean than the two South American coastal countries. However, there does appear to be a link. The warmer atmosphere near the equator in the Pacific Ocean causes upper winds to be stronger at about 30° north latitude. During the winter, these winds blow toward the east over the ocean, moving storms into California. The storms continue moving eastward through the southern United States bringing above-average rainfall. The changed storm track causes the northwest Unites States and British Columbia, Canada, to be drier than normal. The last several El Niño episodes have caused mild, dry winters in Washington, Oregon, Idaho, Montana, and British Columbia.

Many variables affect weather changes, so the link may not be a strong one. The 1993 El Niño is thought by some scientists to have caused the terrible summer Midwest floods in the United States. These are floods that occur only once every 200 to 500 years. Yet the 1993 El Niño was not very strong. Then how could it cause all these dramatic climatic effects? Other variables are suspected, so research scientists continue to look for them.

Scientists still have much to learn about El Niño. They do not know what causes an El Niño, and much research is being done to find out. Recently they discovered that an El Niño-like event occurs in the Indian Ocean. The scientists also believe that the two El Niños have a powerful impact on global weather. The Indian Ocean El Niño occurs simultaneously with the Pacific El Niño. As warmer waters moves from the east coast of Africa to India over a 12- to 18-month period, western Australia, Indonesia, and India experience droughts. So far, the research indicates that El Niños can change the climate for a year or two over the tropics and possibly in North America. The combined influence of the Pacific and Indian Ocean El Niños may extend even farther than is currently known, and that's what research scientists are trying to find out.

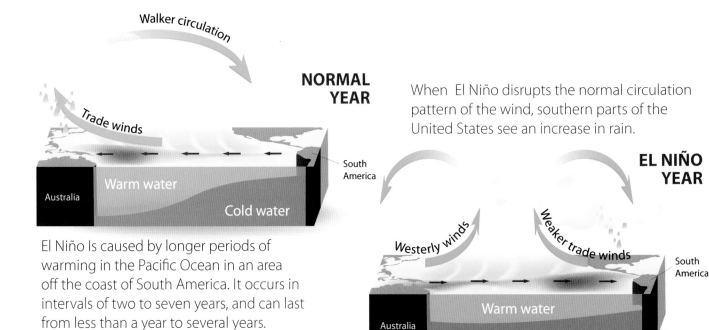

Walker circulation

Trade winds

NORMAL YEAR

Australia

Warm water

Cold water

South America

El Niño Is caused by longer periods of warming in the Pacific Ocean in an area off the coast of South America. It occurs in intervals of two to seven years, and can last from less than a year to several years.

When El Niño disrupts the normal circulation pattern of the wind, southern parts of the United States see an increase in rain.

EL NIÑO YEAR

Westerly winds

Weaker trade winds

Australia

Warm water

Cold water

South America

Oceanic and Atmospheric Cycles

Besides El Niño and its opposite La Niña, scientists have recently discovered that there are several cycles in the oceans and atmosphere that cause small changes in the climate. These cycles or oscillations last anywhere from months to years. Two of the major cycles are the North Atlantic Oscillation and the Pacific Decadal Oscillation.

Pacific Decadal Oscillation

Another major cycle is the very complicated Pacific Decadal Oscillation (PDO). It is measured by differences in sea surface temperatures from the average in the North Pacific Ocean. When the western part of the Pacific Ocean water becomes warm and part of the eastern part cools, the Aleutian Low, a permanent low-pressure area around the Aleutian Islands, is stronger. When this happens, warm, moist air flows more often into the Pacific Northwest, British Columbia, and Alaska. In the other half of the cycle, the opposite pattern is observed, and temperatures are cooler. Such oceanic temperature changes have a cycle of around 20 to 30 years — a decadal time scale. The cause of the PDO is not well known but is a complex interaction between the atmosphere and oceans, which interact with each other.

North Atlantic Oscillation

One of the main cycles is the "North Atlantic Oscillation" (NAO), a climate fluctuation in the North Atlantic that results from a change in air pressure between Iceland and the Azores, islands located about 850 miles (1,350 km) off the coast of Portugal. These pressure fluctuations have a control on the direction and strength of the general west winds and storm tracks. When the pressure difference between the two locations is strong, Europe has more storms from the west with cooler summers and milder, wet winters. The opposite happens when the pressure difference is below average. Other areas around the North Atlantic Ocean are also affected by the NAO, but not as much as in Europe.

The NAO is part of the larger Arctic Oscillation. It is believed by some scientists that the NAO is controlled by changes in ocean properties, especially temperature, which affects the atmosphere. However, it is also possible that the atmosphere changes the ocean properties. Scientists are not sure.

Greenhouse Warming

The greenhouse effect causes the earth to be about 60°F (33°C) warmer than it otherwise would be. That is a good thing, or else most of the earth would be below freezing. It is another provision by God to sustain His creation. The greenhouse effect is 90 to 95 percent caused by water vapor in the atmosphere, with other gases, such as carbon dioxide and methane, contributing less than 5 percent.

Since 1959, scientists have measured the change in carbon dioxide. They have found that carbon dioxide has been steadily rising. We also know that carbon dioxide has been increasing since the late 1800s, based on indirect data, such as tree rings and ice cores. Several sources contribute to this condition. Gasoline and oil are fossil fuels, and when burned they add carbon dioxide to the atmosphere. When rain forests in the tropics are cut down, much of the carbon from the wood and the soil eventually ends up in the atmosphere. It combines with oxygen to make carbon dioxide. Methane has also been increasing. Scientists are fearful that these greenhouse gases will cause the earth to be become much warmer in the future.

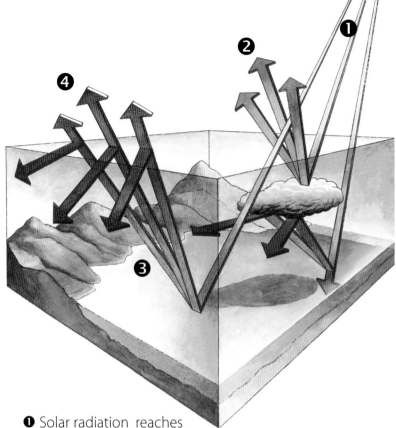

❶ Solar radiation reaches the earth. ❷ Some of the radiation is reflected away while part of it is absorbed. ❸ As the earth's surface releases infrared radiation into the atmosphere. ❹ Some of that is absorbed by greenhouse gases.

The Facts of Global Warming

As stewards of God's creation, we need to be interested in global warming. But first we need to find out the facts according to 1 Thessalonians 5:21: "Examine everything carefully; hold fast to that which is good" (NASB). We need to hold fast to the Bible, God's Word to us, but we need to examine the issue of global warming carefully. Just like weather forecasts need observations to start with, we must gather the observations. There is much information on greenhouse warming that is wrong or greatly exaggerated.

No Consensus

Besides the increase in carbon dioxide and the observation of natural climate cycles, another fact is that there is no consensus of scientists that global warming is a serious threat and that we need to act now, as some advocates claim. One of those advocates is Al Gore, former vice president of the United States, in his exaggerated book, *An Inconvenient Truth*. As of 2014, 31,000 scientists, including more than 9,000 with PhD degrees, have signed a petition online saying global warming is not a serious threat and we have time for unbiased research.

Exaggerated Opinions

From this information has flowed a series of conclusions about how increased carbon dioxide would affect our world. The prospect of several degrees warming fuelled fears that long droughts may occur where most of the world's food is grown. This would result in starvation and wars. A warmer atmosphere would warm the oceans, causing more frequent and much stronger hurricanes. The extra heat could melt part of the Greenland and Antarctic Ice Sheets. The meltwater would result in a higher sea level. Low areas of coastal cities would be flooded. Low wetlands, like the Florida Everglades, would be destroyed, and some species would become extinct. Even the West Antarctic Ice Sheet, grounded well below sea level, might slip into the ocean. Some scientists think that a little warming could start it moving. If the ice sheet slipped into the deep ocean, sea level around the world would rise rapidly 20 feet (6 m). These are frightening warnings for the future climate.

Based on what could happen with greenhouse warming, some scientists tell people that we must act now to prevent these tragedies. Some people say we must spend trillions of dollars to stop the warming, although there is little evidence that we can do anything. The rich countries must aid the poor countries. We must all live simpler lives.

Many exaggerated statements have been made by advocates of catastrophic global warming. One top government official has stated that one billion people could die by 2020. Others have said that the Antarctic continent or the Arctic will be the only habitable areas on earth by century's end. Others claim that global warming is causing huge storms.

Even a new term has been coined that seems designed to scare people, and that is the "polar vortex." This actually is a strong low-pressure upper trough in the middle and upper atmosphere that draws Arctic air down into the United States from Alaska and Canada. Actually, it is nothing unusual in the field of meteorology. Upper troughs move through North America regularly, being stronger in winter and weaker in summer. They vary from weak to strong. It is nothing unusual.

Slight Temperature Rise

Another fact is we have also observed that temperatures have warmed on the average on the globe. Temperature records that go back to about 1850 show an increase of about 1°F (0.6°C). That is all that is claimed. Most of the glaciers, very sensitive to climate change, have shrunk since about 1900. Advocates are worried more about the future warming inferred from climate simulations.

However, these temperature records are in error on the warm side. One of the many errors is a result of the "heat island" effect. As cities grow, more sunshine is absorbed by houses, buildings, and concrete. The absorbed sunshine warms the atmosphere. Because of the heat island effect, Phoenix, Arizona, has warmed over 6°F (3°C). Long temperature records in or near growing cities would show warming that did not occur in the surrounding countryside. Advocates have mostly filtered the heat island effect out of the temperature records, but not totally. Other errors are changing the location of instrument shelters, placing shelters near heat sources, and changing instruments. Dr. Robert Balling, a professor at Arizona State University, is skeptical of catastrophic global warming. He believes that about 30 to 40 percent of the claimed temperature rise is wrong, so the real rise is probably around 0.6°F (0.4°C). He believes the greenhouse warming is true, but small. Balling has compiled the available data into a book named *The Heated Debate.**

---

* *The Heated Debate: Greenhouse Predictions Versus Climate Reality* Robert C. Balling,
  (San Francisco, CA; Pacific Research
  Institute for Public Policy, 1992)

Brazil Forest

Deforestation

Deforestation Exaggerated

Some environmentalists have claimed that huge amounts of tropical forests have been clear cut, especially in Brazil. However, satellite pictures have shown that these estimates for Brazil are much too high. Moreover, advocates seem to forget that forests grow back. Alan Grainger stated in a prestigious scientific journal* that there has been only little change in the amount of tropical forests — if "reforestation" is taken into account.

---

* Alan Grainger, "Difficulties in Tracking the Long-term Global Trend in Tropical Forest Area," Proceedings of the National Academy of Science 105(2):818–823, 2008.

Computer Climate Simulations Exaggerated

Another fact is that computer simulations of the climate are exaggerated. By studying computer experiments, scientists estimate that a doubling of carbon dioxide would cause earth's average temperature to increase from 3 to 11°F (1.7 to 6°C). These climate simulations vary a lot because the atmosphere is very complicated. The computer experiments that have predicted very warm temperatures for an increase in carbon dioxide are flawed. Many processes in the atmosphere are too complex to put accurately into a computer. One of these is cloud processes. Other sources of error are solar and infrared radiation values, the snow-aging effect, and oceanic processes.

However, we have observations of nature that demonstrate the computer climate simulations are greatly exaggerated. We have observed an increase in carbon dioxide and temperature for over 100 years, and by examining the detailed record, we can estimate the amount of rise in the future. Carbon dioxide has risen more than 30 percent, and when you add the other greenhouse gases up, it is like increasing carbon dioxide another 30 percent. Let's call them "carbon dioxide equivalency units." Therefore, the total rise in carbon dioxide equivalency units has been about 60 percent. After reducing the heating biases in the temperature record, such an increase in greenhouse gases has caused only a 0.6°F (0.4°C) temperature rise. So if we double carbon dioxide equivalency units,

making it a 100 percent increase, the temperature rise should be only 1°F (0.6°C). Even the smallest estimate of a rise by climate simulations of 3°F (1.7°C) is three times too high. We should accept observations before flawed computer simulations.

When we look at natural process of climate change from the sun, we find that much of our recent global warming can be attributed to the sunspot cycle. Remember that we had the Medieval Warm Period and the Little Ice Age before the recent warming. Also, when we look at the detailed changes in carbon dioxide, temperature, and the sunspot cycle for the 20th century, we can see that natural processes account for more than 50 percent of the recent global warming. We have had carbon dioxide increasing throughout the 20th century. However, we had a major rise in temperature between 1910 and 1940, while carbon dioxide was increasing only a little. Between about 1945 and 1975, we actually had global cooling! This occurred at a time when carbon dioxide was increasing substantially. From 1998 to 2014, we have had little change in temperature around the globe, while carbon dioxide has been increasing dramatically. However, these changes in temperature can be related better to the sunspot cycles. Therefore, if natural processes have caused more than 50 percent of the warming, the man-made part can be reduced from 0.6°F (0.4°C) to 0.3°F (0.2°C) with a doubling of carbon dioxide being only 0.5°F (0.3°C).

İs Global Warming İncreasing Storms?

There have been a lot of scare tactics in the global warming debate. One of them is the increased number and/or intensity of storms caused by global warming. First of all, it is very difficult to make such a claim since we would have to know how a bit of temperature increase caused a particular storm. We have had strong storms since at least the end of the Flood. Second, statistics do not back up these advocates. Roger Pielke Jr., the son of well-known atmospheric scientist Roger Pielke Sr., has compiled statistics of storms over the past. He published it all in the book *The Climate Fix.* * He has concluded that over the long-term there has been no change in (1) hurricane landfalls, (2) droughts, (3) floods, (4) tornadoes or thunderstorms, (5) East Coast winter storms, (6) heat waves, and (7) cold spells.

* Roger Pielke Jr., *The Climate Fix: What Scientists and Politicians Won't Tell You about Global Warming*, (New York: Basic Books) 2010. pg 184-185

Climate Change Causes Environmental Problems

Sometimes a slight change in climate can cause the environment to change. Such changes may be caused by man. Such examples include increased pollution in valleys during winter that causes health problems. Another example is the spewing of smoke and other pollutants from cars and factories that can cause acid rain. A third example is the addition of compounds of the element chlorine into the air that have caused chemical changes in the stratosphere, namely the loss of ozone.

Conclusions

It is important to study the data long and carefully before we make changes in our world that would greatly affect our political and economic system. It is important to gather the facts, first. Global warming has been slight and will continue to be slight. More than half of global warming is caused by natural cycles of climate change. We have time for more unbiased research.

The Ozone Hole

Ozone is formed in the stratosphere when sunlight strikes oxygen. This ozone layer protects the earth from harmful ultraviolet rays. Without the ozone layer, we would all die. The little bit of ultraviolet light that does make it through the atmosphere kills excess bacteria and produces vitamin D in our skin. The ozone layer is another one of God's provisions for the protection of life on earth.

Many scientists fear that the ozone layer is decreasing due to chlorine compounds and other chemicals that humans are putting into the air. Chlorofluorocarbons from spray cans, air conditioners, and refrigerators are blamed. These chemicals break down very slowly, so they can be spread with time into the stratosphere. Scientists have found and measured these chemicals high in the atmosphere.

It is well-known that if the ozone layer decreases, more ultraviolet light will reach the earth's surface. If this happened, there would be more cases of skin cancer and cataracts. Some scientists guess that increased ultraviolet light would also harm plants and animals, including the plankton in the sea.

In 1985, scientists discovered what is called an ozone hole around the South Pole. The ozone does not disappear; it just thins out for a short time. Another minor ozone hole was discovered over the Arctic area of the Northern Hemisphere.

Scientists have been trying to estimate how much the ozone around the world has decreased in the past and will decrease in the future. Although their estimates vary, they agree that the ozone layer has already decreased several percent. Early estimates for the future have ranged from a 3 percent to an 18 percent decrease in ozone by the year 2050 — if we did not do anything about it. Scientists have also spent much time measuring the amount of ultraviolet light that has slipped through the ozone layer. These measurements have been chaotic. In the Swiss Alps between 1980 and 1989, scientists measured about a 6 percent increase in ultraviolet radiation. Some have said there has been no change in ozone in cities because of pollution and haze absorbing the harmful rays.

The ozone hole has more scientific backing than the predictions of global warming. That is why countries got together and banned chlorofluorocarbons in what is called the 1987 Montreal Protocol treaty. Ever since about 1990, the total ozone has been observed to recover about 10 percent.[*] So the ozone hole should slowly diminish over the decades and be less of a threat to the environment.

---

[*] T.G. Shepherd et al., "Reconciliation of Halogen-induced Ozone Loss with the Total-column Ozone Record", Nature Geoscience 7:443–449, 2014.

The purple area represents the area where the least amount of ozone is found in the stratosphere; the other colors denote levels of ozone present in those areas. The ozone tends to thin out in the spring, September, and October in the Southern Hemisphere.

Cause of the Ozone Hole

In trying to figure out the cause of the ozone hole, scientists have discovered that nature is very complex. Many variables (facts that can make a difference) affect the thickness of the ozone layer. They found that the amount of ozone in the stratosphere goes in cycles. One cycle is a 2-year cycle. It is caused by the switching of the stratospheric winds over the equator. Another cycle is an 11-year sunspot cycle.

Another variable is how the air circulates in the stratosphere. This movement sometimes mixes air from the mid-latitudes into the polar latitudes. The air in the mid-latitudes has more ozone, so when the winds carry the mid-latitude air to near the pole, ozone is added. This causes the amount of ozone around the poles to vary a lot.

Volcanic dust and gases affect ozone. The volcanoes add chlorine to the stratosphere, and this added chlorine affects the chemical balance.

Scientists have also discovered that the chemical reaction between chlorofluorocarbons, the air, and other chemicals is very complicated. Some reactions increase ozone and some decrease it. The chemicals believed to destroy ozone often do not react at all.

But these chemicals will react when the stratosphere is cooler than normal. A special cloud forms if the temperatures are cold enough; they are called polar stratospheric clouds, which is a combination of ice and frozen nitric acid. Only near the poles where there is no winter sunshine are the temperatures in the stratosphere cold enough to form this type of cloud. When sunlight hits these clouds in late winter or spring, it triggers a reaction with chlorofluorocarbons that thins out the ozone forming an "ozone hole." The effect is mainly in the Southern Hemisphere where temperatures are colder in the stratosphere in winter than over the high latitudes of the Northern Hemisphere. However, there is a slight thinning of the ozone over the Arctic in early spring, which does not appear to be much of a threat.

Ozone and the Origin of Life

Ozone also presents a serious problem for those scientists who believe life evolved billions of years ago from chemicals in the ocean. They call this ocean full of chemicals the "soupy sea." They believe the earth's atmosphere had no oxygen. Life could not evolve from chemicals with oxygen in the atmosphere. But, with no oxygen, there would be no protective layer of ozone. Ozone is made from oxygen. With no ozone, ultraviolet light would strongly bombard the surface of the earth, penetrating about 100 feet (30 m) into the soupy sea. The ultraviolet light would kill any developing life. Of course all of this assumes there really was a soupy sea and that life can get started from non-life, major assumptions with no backing.

So, the evolutionary-uniformitarian model advocates have a problem with their theory. They cannot evolve life with oxygen in the atmosphere, and they cannot do it without oxygen. Why not then conclude life had to have been created by God? This is a good question for them. The lack of ozone is just one of the many problems with the idea that life evolved from chemicals in a soupy sea.

11 | God, Creation and You

God is the Creator (Colossians 1:16). He has placed us in charge of His wonderful creation. Genesis 1:28 says that people are to "be fruitful and increase in number; fill the earth and subdue it. Rule over the fish of the sea and the birds of the air and over every living creature that moves on the ground" (NIV). Indeed, we are in charge, and we do rule over all the animals and the plants.

However, some people misinterpret this verse and claim it gives people permission to harm the environment and destroy the earth. They blame Christians for many of our environmental problems and for possibly changing the future climate. This verse does not mean that we are to destroy God's wonderful creation.

You can go back to Genesis and read verse 2:15 which says: "The Lord God took the man and put him in the garden of Eden to work it and keep it." Although we are in charge of God's creation, we have been given the responsibility to take care of it.

Words to Know

Creation	Pantheist
Environmentalist	steward
Theory of Evolution	

Level 1 | Level 2 | Level 3

We are Stewards of God's Creation

Therefore, we should be concerned about climate change, the ozone layer, and air pollution. We should not be polluting the earth ourselves, and we should support those who are trying to fix environmental problems. However, we must have a reasonably clear idea of what the problem is before we can fix it. We need to gather the facts. Too many people have wanted to spend billions of dollars to stop climate change. They have urged us to act before we have understood the problem. Further research on greenhouse warming shows there is a problem, but it is not as serious as the doomsayers proclaim. The decrease of the ozone layer is a more serious problem and has better scientific support. So there has been more effort to decrease the ozone loss.

Misguided Ideas

Some of the people who urge action to save the environment may have other reasons besides concern for the environment. Some urge that we live simpler lives. A few claim we need to go "back to nature." They say we will stop polluting the planet if we drastically change our lifestyle. However, very poor countries, where the people live so-called simple lives, have severe environmental problems. The "simple lives" of the Indians in Brazil cause them to cut down and burn their rain forests. The countries that lived under socialism in the former Soviet Union also have severe environmental problems. So living "simple lives" will not necessarily bring about a better environment. In fact, the environment of technologically advanced North America has some of the cleanest air, water, and streets of any area in the world.

A few environmentalists, called pantheists, believe animals, trees, the environment, and the earth are god. If everything is god, why should we even be concerned about pollution and the environment? If the earth were god, it could take care of itself. Pantheism seems to be anti-environmental.

Many environmentalists try to convince us that man is a risen animal. They believe we have no more right to the earth than other animals. Their basic assumption is the theory of evolution. However, animals have no concern for their environment. How can the belief that we are risen animals really help the environmental problem? They do not understand that mankind is made in God's image and likeness. The creation was made by God. Therefore, we should respect and take care of God's creation.

Most environmentalists are genuinely concerned for the environment. Some are committed Christians who have been led to become involved in environmental issues. Their motivation is love for God's creation and concern for His people and animals. As Christians, we should be able to join together with non-Christians to solve legitimate environmental issues.

The Christian realizes the most serious pollution problem is sin. It is man who does evil, including polluting the environment. Unless we deal with the evil in man's heart by bringing people to Jesus, there is little hope for progress toward a better environment. The Christian should be involved in eliminating both kinds of pollution.

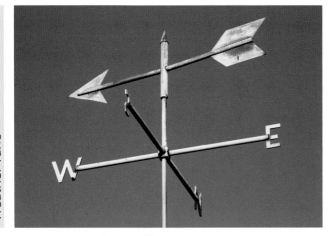

Weather Vane

A weather vane is used to show the direction of the wind. They are often used as a decorative item for yards, barns, sheds and even some houses and other buildings. They were also popular for churches in the 9th century, relating it to the story of St. Peter. A weather vane consists of four directional pieces that represent north, south, east, and west. This part remains stationary, while the pointer – which moves freely – turns to indicate wind direction.

Thermometer

Thermometers are used to measure temperature. Like other instruments widely used to gather weather-related data, a common standard for these measurements are used around the world. There are two main elements of a thermometer: a temperature sensor and a numerical scale to show temperature. Mercury is used in thermometers because it is a liquid at room temperature and produces a noticeable change when the temperature changes.

Rain Gauge & thermometer

A rain gauge gathers and measures the amount of precipitation over a specific period of time. For instance, when you are watching the weather before or after a storm, the meteorologist will often say how much rain is expected to fall or how much the rainfall total was in the last 24 hours or even the current month. Records of rainfall were kept in ancient cultures in Greece, Korea, and India.

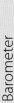

Barometer

Barometers are used to find out the atmospheric pressure, which is the force from the weight of the air in the atmosphere exerted upon the Earth's surface. By measuring the change in pressure over a period of time, you can do a short-term forecast of the weather. For example, if the pressure rises quickly in a short time, this could correlate to clearer skies.

Glossary

arid – a dry climate lacking moisture. ... 8, 75

atmosphere – the body of gasses surrounding the earth. ... 3-5, 7, 9-11, 13-15, 17-18, 21-23, 28, 34-36, 50, 54, 57, 61, 66, 68, 70, 77-78, 81, 83-88, 90-91

avalanche – a rapid flow of snow down a sloping surface ... 8, 75

axis – an imaginary straight line through the center of the earth on which it rotates. ... 4, 6, 10, 61

ball lightning – a glowing ball of red, orange, or yellow light found during a thunderstorm ... 68, 72

barometer – a weather instrument used to measure the pressure of the atmosphere. ... 8, 19, 57

blizzard – a very heavy snowstorm with violent winds. ... 4-5, 60, 63-64

bogs – soft, waterlogged ground such as a march. ... 74-75, 80

carbon dioxide – a colorless, odorless gas formed during respiration, combustion, and organic decomposition. ... 4, 7, 18, 78, 86-88

chinook winds – foehn winds that are mild, gusty west winds found along the east slopes of the Rocky Mountains. ... 68, 70-71

cirrus clouds – a high altitude cloud made of ice crystals that appear thin, white, and feathery. ... 20

climate – the weather conditions that are particular to a certain area, such as wind, precipitation, and temperature. ... 3-4, 6, 15-17, 61, 69, 74-89, 92-93

cold front – a boundary of cold air, usually moving from the north or west, which is displacing the warm air. ... 13, 20, 29, 31, 66, 73, 95

condensation – the act of water vapor changing from a gas to a liquid. ... 8, 20-21, 35, 45, 71, 95

convection clouds – clouds that occur in a rising up-draft, usually when the sun's radiation warms the earth. This causes the water vapor to condense. ... 20, 23, 95

creation – the formation of everything by God ... 3, 5, 21, 60, 76, 86, 92-93, 95

dew point – the temperature at which air becomes saturated and dew forms. ... 8, 13, 30, 95

Doppler radar – a special type of radar used to track severe weather by detecting wind speed and direction. ... 8, 14-15, 18, 51

downdraft – a downward current of air. ... 32, 35, 41, 44, 46-47, 54

dust devil – a relatively long-lived whirlwind on the ground formed on a clear, hot day. ... 40, 45

El Niño – a warm current from the west that replaces the cool ocean current along Peru and Ecuador. ... 82-85

electricity – a moving electric charge, such as in a thunderstorm. ... 32-33, 36-38, 57, 64, 72

electrons – a subatomic particle with a negative electrical charge. ... 32, 37-38, 95

environment – the surrounding circumstances or conditions around us. ... 74, 78, 89-90, 92-93

environmentalist – someone concerned with the environment, usually an activist trying to change what is believed to be harmful human activities. ... 92

equator – an imaginary line dividing the northern and southern hemispheres. ... 8, 11, 16-17, 45, 52-54, 61, 82, 84, 91

evaporation – to change into a vapor such as the evaporation of water by the warming of the sun. ... 20-21, 30, 44, 54, 73, 79

flash flood – a flood caused by thunderstorm that deposits an unusual amount of rain on a particular area. ... 40-42

foehn wind – a dry, warm downslope wind on the lee side of a mountain range. ... 70-71

fog – clouds that form on the surface of the ground. ... 20, 23, 30-31, 67

fossil fuels – coal and oil derived from the remains of plant and animal organisms. ... 82, 86

frostbite – localized damage to skin and tissues due to freezing ... 60, 65

funnel cloud – a rotating whirlwind below a cloud that has not yet touched the ground ... 40, 45-46, 51

greenhouse warming – the phenomena of a steady, gradual rise of temperatures due to the increase of carbon dioxide in the atmosphere. This could a result in natural catastrophes such as droughts, flooding, and a meltdown of the ice sheets. ... 86-87, 93

hailstones – precipitation in the form of ice and hard snow pellets. ... 40, 42-43, 47

heat island effect – the warming effect in cities, compared to rural areas, caused by human activities. ... 87

humid – a weather condition containing a large amount of moisture or water vapor. ... 20, 75, 78

hurricane – the strongest storm found in the tropic, with heavy rain and winds of 75 mph or greater. ... 15, 18, 52-59, 61, 70, 89

hypothermia – a condition in which the body temperature drops below that required for biological functions. ... 60, 65, 67, 95

Ice Age – a period of time marked by extensive glaciers on the face of the earth ... 4, 6, 74-75, 78-82, 88, 95-96

ice cap – an extensive covering of ice and snow. ... 8, 95

ice jam – the buildup of water caused by a blockage of ice. ... 60

ice storm – a storm caused by rain falling into a lower atmosphere that is below freezing. ... 60

Intertropical Convergence Zone – area near the equator where winds from different directions merge or mix. ... 52-53, 61

inversion – a condition in which the atmospheric temperature increases upward ... 31, 60, 66

La Niña – an ocean/atmospheric phenomenon that is the opposite of El Niño ... 82-83, 85

lake-effect snowstorm – a snowstorm produced when cool air moves over long expanses of warm water, evaporating much moisture, and precipitating on downwind shores. ... 73